The Invisible Threshold

Other Books of Interest from St. Augustine's Press

Gabriel Marcel, *Homo Viator: Introduction to the Metaphysics of Hope*

Gabriel Marcel, *Man against Mass Society*

Gabriel Marcel, *The Mystery of Being: Volume 1, Reflection and Mystery*

Gabriel Marcel, *The Mystery of Being: Volume 2, Faith and Reality*

Gabriel Marcel, *Thou Shall Not Die*

Brendan Sweetman (editor), *A Gabriel Marcel Reader*

Max Picard, *The Flight from God*

Gerard V. Bradley, *Unquiet Americans*

James V. Schall, *The Praise of 'Sons of Bitches':*
On the Worship of God by Fallen Men

Gary M. Bouchard, *Southwell's Sphere:*
The Influence of England's Secret Poet

Charles R. Embry and Glenn Hughes (editors), *Timelessness of Proust:*
Reflections on In Search of Lost Time

Frederic Raphael and Joseph Epstein, *Where Were We?*

Marion Montgomery, *With Walker Percy at the Tupperware Party:*
In Company with Flannery O'Connor, T. S. Eliot, and Others

Étienne Gilson, *Theology and the Cartesian Doctrine of Freedom*

Josef Kleutgen, S.J., *Pre-Modern Philosophy Defended*

Edward Feser, *The Last Superstition: A Refutation of the New Atheism*

Ernest A. Fortin, A.A., *Christianity and Philosophical Culture in the Fifth*
Century: The Controversy about the Human Soul in the West

Peter Kreeft, *Ethics for Beginners: 52 "Big Ideas" from 32 Great Minds*

Peter Kreeft, *The Platonic Tradition*

Peter Kreeft, *Socrates' Children: The 100 Greatest Philosophers*

Josef Pieper, *The Christian Idea of Man*

Josef Pieper, *Don't Worry about Socrates: Three Plays for Television*

Karl Rahner, *Encounters with Silence*

The Invisible Threshold

Two Plays by Gabriel Marcel

Edited by
Brendan Sweetman
Maria Traub
Geoffrey Karabin

Translated by Maria Traub

ST. AUGUSTINE'S PRESS
South Bend, Indiana

Manufactured in the United States of America.

1 2 3 4 5 6   25 24 23 22 21 20 19

Library of Congress Control Number: 2019950324

∞ The paper used in this publication meets the minimum requirements of the American National Standard for Information Sciences - Permanence of Paper for Printed Materials, ANSI Z39.48-1984.

St. Augustine's Press
www.staugustine.net

Table of Contents

INTRODUCTION

I

French philosopher and dramatist Gabriel Marcel (1888–1973), who belonged to the movement of French existentialism, is one of the most insightful thinkers of the twentieth century. Unlike some of his contemporaries who took existentialism in an atheistic, even nihilist direction, Marcel is usually classified as a theistic existentialist who gives priority to the themes of hope, fidelity and faith in the human search for meaning in a challenging world. Although a distinguished thinker, Marcel never held a formal position as a professor of philosophy but worked primarily as a respected theater critic and reviewer. He wrote for more than forty years for various French periodicals, magazines, and newspapers, including *L'Europe nouvelle, Nouvelles littéraires* and *Temps Présent*. He so loved theater that he went to several plays a week, right up until shortly before his death.

Marcel wrote seventeen major works of philosophy, which have been translated into English and other languages, as well as a large number of articles, review essays, and opinion pieces. Also a playwright, he wrote more than thirty plays, including tragedies and comedies, many of which were staged in theaters in Paris, Germany, Belgium, England, and Ireland. About sixteen of his plays have been translated into English, including the two in the present volume, and several have been performed at various venues in the United States.

In Marcel's work, dramatic art comes first in both a chronological and an intellectual sense. He has acknowledged that his plays deal with challenging experiences and issues of contention that arise between people, especially families, in day-to-day life, and has described his general style as "post-Ibsen," because it involves a sense of realism, depictions of passion and sincerity, and a sense of moral duty, all evident in his characters and themes. He also admits that some of the situations and events depicted in his drama are taken from his own experience, as one would expect of any writer. Marcel's plays rarely provide complete or settled answers to the difficulties they confront, but suggest possibilities both of interpretation and in terms of the choices humans must make in life. They allow audiences (and readers) not only to arrive at their own conclusions, but through the experience of this art form to feel the echo of the dramatic action in their own lives, and so provoke both insight and critical reflection on the dramatic themes.

In theater, Marcel believed that one could recreate through the medium of art profound human experiences close to the way in which they actually occur in human life; later one could reflect on such experiences in a philosophical way, but the echo of these experiences in one's own life would play a large role in how one came to respond to them and to understand them. Marcel scholar and theater expert, K. R. Hanley, puts the point very well: "Theater shows the way life's challenges, conflicts, and questions touch people's lives concretely. Dramas portray how people's lives are affected incarnately, that is bodily, spiritually, affectively, and consciously by life's crucial events. Since the theater shows people's responses to the impact of significant events that affect their lives, it can be a highly valuable if not indispensable way of accessing Marcel's philosophic reflection."[1] Only later would Marcel in his mature philosophical work return to several of the important themes in his drama as he worked out the meaning of central human experiences, not just for the human condition, but also for what they reveal about the nature of philosophizing about the human condition. Marcel's dramatic works are therefore a very important part of his overall philosophical project.

II

Marcel has often suggested that philosophy is not only an academic exercise but also something of a quest. This means that the individual is involved in a unique, personal way in the experience of philosophizing, of working

---

1   K. R. Hanley (ed.), *Two One Act Plays by Gabriel Marcel* (Lanham, MD: University Press of America, 1986), pp. xviii–xix.

through philosophical questions that arise in one's own life situation. As Marcel puts it, the individual is often *involved* in the philosophical question being asked in such a way that if one treats the question as an abstraction and seeks a universal solution then something is lost. This is because often the "abstract" question is not the question one begins with; the question one begins with is usually prompted by a person's individual situation and unique experiences. The idea that philosophy involves a personal quest on the part of the inquirer is a theme of the existentialist philosophical movement in general. Several philosophers in that movement including Heidegger, Jaspers, and Merleau Ponty, held that there is an experiential aspect to philosophizing that conceptual knowledge, understood as an abstraction from experience, and as seeking universal solutions that can apply to any human being regardless of their concrete situation in existence, can miss. And so the theme of experience and reflection becomes key throughout existentialist thought, as it is in the work of Marcel. As a result, these philosophers place a large role on the personal experiences of the individual when engaged in the task of philosophizing, and this is of the first importance. Various philosophers develop this point in different ways, but I think that Marcel's way of developing it is one of the most profound and the most convincing.

Marcel is well known for distinguishing in his thought between two realms of knowledge, problem and mystery, which correspond to the distinction between conceptual thinking and experience. By the term primary reflection Marcel is referring to the realm of conceptual knowledge. This realm is concerned with abstract thinking, logical distinctions and theoretical analysis; it is a realm where we seek solutions to ordinary everyday problems that arise in our day to day lives. Marcel understands a "problem" as a temporary difficulty, as a puzzle, that requires a solution that is available for everybody.[2] A problem of this sort presupposes a community in which the problem can be publicly formulated, tackled, and hopefully solved. Problems require solutions that are universal in nature, meaning that they apply to everyone and can be understood and utilized by everyone in the same way. Examples of this type of thinking would include repairing a car

2   See Marcel, *The Mystery of Being, Vol.1*, trans. G. S. Fraser (Chicago: Regnery, 1951), p. 4ff.

engine, furnishing an office space, or seeking a cure for an illness. This realm of thinking is also the realm in which most academic disciplines do their work, including science, theology, and even philosophy itself. However, Marcel argues, there is a difficulty that applies to all thinking that takes place in the realm of primary reflection. This type of thinking is unable to capture accurately a whole realm of experience, which he refers to as the realm of mystery. The difficulty arises because primary reflection by its nature requires a move to abstraction, and it is in this very move that the personal experience of the subject who is doing the conceptual thinking is removed and set aside so that abstract functional solutions can be obtained. Marcel is not trying to denigrate primary reflection by means of this criticism. He recognizes that it is an essential part of human life, and does not object to primary reflection in itself; he objects only to any attempt to make it the paradigm way of understanding the nature of knowledge. This mistake with regard to primary reflection is characteristic of modernity: a prevailing attitude today is that it is possible to find a solution to all human concerns by means of this method, yet nothing could be further from the truth.

Marcel holds that there is a deeper realm of mystery that has a quite important revelatory role in philosophy. Ralph McInerny has recognized the importance of this realm in Marcel, noting that, "If he had done nothing else, his success in this matter would constitute a major contribution to philosophy."[3] The realm of mystery is not to be understood in a religious or mystical sense, nor is Marcel trying to suggest that it is an unknowable realm. As McInerny notes, Marcel believes that both art and philosophy deal with mystery, rather than art dealing with mystery and philosophy dealing with problems. The realm of mystery, for Marcel, is best understood as a realm where the distinction between the concept and the object it wishes to capture breaks down, where the questioner is involved in the question in such a way that if the questioner becomes detached from the question in an act of conceptual abstraction, then the question will be changed, even distorted, and the questioner is then thinking about a different question: "A

---

3   Ralph McInerny, "Introduction" in *Gabriel Marcel's Perspectives on The Broken World*, trans. and ed. K. R. Hanley (Milwaukee, WI: Marquette University Press, 1998), p.10.

mystery is something in which I am myself involved, and it can therefore only be thought of *as a sphere where the distinction between subject and object, between what is in me and what is before me, loses its meaning and its initial validity.*[4] Marcel believes that the realm of mystery includes ordinary concrete human situations that involve experiences of love, hope, fidelity and faith, which are defining for human beings, and which are part of the essence of what it means to be human. This realm also includes other areas of profound philosophical significance such as the experience of the unity of body and mind, and our experience of our own concrete existence in the world. The reason these latter two are of profound significance is because they enable Marcel to develop a strong critique of the approach to several philosophical issues that emerged from the influential work of René Descartes. For example, Descartes is famous for his program of methodic doubt and for developing arguments for skepticism, but Marcel thinks that Descartes started from an *arbitrary* split between the self and the world, which then enabled him to generate an artificial problem of skepticism. Descartes overlooked the limitations of the realm of primary reflection, and mistakenly took it to be the paradigm way to knowledge.

Marcel uses the example of the experience of evil to illustrate the distinction between problem and mystery. Philosophers, he says, discuss the topic of evil from the point of view of considering it as a problem, and the topic is usually referred to in the philosophical and theological literature by specialists as "the problem of evil." The "problem" is how to reconcile the existence of evil in the world with the all-good and all-powerful nature of God. Philosophers and theologians propose various abstract solutions that are meant to show logically how God and evil could co-exist, and why God might have allowed evil into the world. While the discussion is not without value, Marcel holds that it is not a consideration of the experience of evil, of how evil affects a person in their own lives, and how one might cope with it. In fact, this latter experience cannot be captured in conceptual knowledge, he believes, because conceptual knowledge requires that we abstract from our personal experience, and pursue an objective, detached line of argument, and this requires precisely that we leave our experience out

4   Marcel, *Being and Having*, trans. K. Farrer (Boston: Beacon Press, 1951), p.117 (emphasis in original).

of the discussion. So the very phenomenon we are trying to understand—the experience of evil—is precluded by the move to abstraction. The discussion of the problem of evil can be helpful, but it is not a discussion of the experience of evil, nor does it take the place of trying to cope with the experience, a mistake academic philosophers in particular make. Marcel is arguing *philosophically* then for a return to ordinary experience.

It is in this context that Marcel introduces the notion of secondary reflection, one of his more difficult concepts. He believes that secondary reflection can help us recover the realm of mystery, as expressed in this passage:

> The recognition of mystery, on the other hand, is an essentially positive act of the mind, the supremely positive act in virtue of which all positivity may perhaps be strictly defined. In this sphere everything seems to go on as if I found myself acting on an intuition which I possess without immediately knowing myself to possess it—an intuition which cannot be, strictly speaking, self-conscious and which can grasp itself only through the modes of experience in which its image is reflected, and which it lights up by being thus reflected in them. The essential metaphysical step would then consist in a reflection upon this reflection. By means of this, thought *stretches out* toward the recovery of an intuition which otherwise loses itself in proportion as it is exercised.[5]

Thomas Michaud has argued that the best way to understand secondary reflection is in its correlation with the problem/mystery distinction. Secondary reflection, according to Michaud, is "a reflection on an intuitive encounter with mystery: a philosophical reflection which 'lives off' a blinded and mute intuition of a mystery of existence and which can illumine and articulate such an intuition to express a philosophically intelligible and satisfying account of the nature of the mystery."[6] Secondary reflection helps

---

5   *Ibid.*, p.118.
6   See Thomas Michaud, "Secondary Reflection and Marcelian Anthropology," *Philosophy Today*, Vol. 34 (1990), pp. 222–28; also Brendan Sweetman, *The Vision of Gabriel Marcel* (Amsterdam: Brill, 2008), pp. 55–60.

us to reach beyond primary reflection, according to Michaud, and, crucially, provides reflective insight into those experiences that are beyond primary reflection. Very important, Michaud also points out that secondary reflection is not only intelligible, but satisfying, at least to the extent that we can identify the experiences and recognize their value. Secondary refection, therefore, does not invite us into an area of total mystery, and so allows us to avoid irrationalism and mysticism.

So I think the most accurate characterization of the concept is that secondary reflection can be understood as *both* the act of critical reflection on primary reflection, *and* the process of recovery of the "mysteries of being." Secondary reflection begins as the *act* of critical reflection (a "second" reflection) on ordinary conceptual thinking (primary reflection). This "second" or critical reflection enables the philosopher to discover that the categories of primary reflection are not adequate to provide a true account of the nature of the self, or of the self's most profound experiences. In this case, secondary reflection does include ordinary reflection, but with the crucial difference that, unlike ordinary reflection, it is a critical reflection directed *at the nature of thought itself.* This first move of secondary reflection then progresses by bringing the human subject out of the realm of the conceptual into the realm of actual experience. Marcel further suggests that the act of secondary reflection culminates in a realization or in an assurance of the realm of mystery. What is this assurance? It is a kind of intuitive grasp or experiential insight into various experiences which are non-conceptual, and which conceptual knowledge can never *fully* express. The concept of secondary reflection opens us to a new dimension, the realm of being, or the realm of the unity of experience. The realm of being, or of mystery, cannot be deduced in the logical sense from the structure of thought; in fact, as he indicates in the passage above, it is the *guide* (the "intuition") of reflective thought.[7]

Marcel illustrates these points with many examples. One to which he frequently returns is that of the experience of fidelity, or faithfulness in human relationships. His main point about fidelity is that a precise rational analysis of the experience of fidelity is not possible. Fidelity appears to

---

7   I have discussed these notions in more detail in my *The Vision of Gabriel Marcel*, op. cit., which informs my discussion here.

have an unconditional element to it that is very difficult to capture in terms of a definition or in terms of trying to state necessary and sufficient conditions for the experience. We recognize the inadequacy of our description or any stated criteria for fidelity in the face of the experience of fidelity. We might, for example, think that one basic necessary condition is that the person we wish to be faithful to must at least be a living person, but Marcel believes that we can easily imagine cases where we should show fidelity to a lost loved one. Yet despite these conceptual difficulties, we can recognize and appreciate the experience of fidelity quite easily when we are in the presence of fidelity.

Marcel agrees with many thinkers of the past that human life has a religious dimension, though he was usually reluctant to link this claim too closely with any denomination, or to expound the strong religious sensibilities in his work in any kind of clear way. In 1929, at the age of forty, Marcel converted to Catholicism. He had just published a review of a novel (*Souffrance du chrétien*) by the French Catholic writer François Mauriac. Mauriac recognized that the review appealed to concerns about human nature and morality that indicated Marcel's acceptance of central Catholic themes concerning forgiveness, moral character, and the religious justification of the moral order. Mauriac wrote to Marcel asking him whether he ought not to join the Catholic Church. Marcel noted that at this point in his life he was enjoying "a period of calm and equilibrium," leading him to treat Mauriac's request as prophetic, saying "he was but a spokesman and the call came from much higher up." It was as though a more than human voice was questioning him, asking him if he could "really persevere indefinitely in that equivocal position of yours?" It was as if the voice said to him: "Is it even honest to continue to think and to speak like someone who believes in the faith of others and who is convinced that this faith is everything but illusion, but who nevertheless does not resolve to take it unto himself? Is there not a sort of equivocation here that must be definitively dispelled; is it not like a leap before which you are obliged to decide?"[8] Marcel answered his own questions and Mauriac's request in the affirmative, and, although his conversion did

8   Marcel, "An Autobiographical Essay," in Paul A. Schilpp and Lewis Hahn (eds.), *The Philosophy of Gabriel Marcel* (La Salle, IL: Open Court, 1984), p. 29.

not change his philosophy in any significant way (an indication that Mauriac's reading of Marcel had been correct), it did cause him to explore the ways that ordinary human experiences, especially moral experiences, call forth the realm of the transcendent in human life. Marcel's conversion is testimony to the fact that religious themes dominated his work from the beginning, and confirm Seymour Cain's observation that "From the beginning of his philosophical career, Marcel's main interest has been the interpretation of religious experience, that is, of the relation between man and ultimate reality."[9]

Although not interested in philosophy of religion in the traditional sense, Marcel does provide a number of indirect arguments in his work for God's existence. In particular, he holds that the profound experiences, such as fidelity, that he has identified as belonging to the realm of mystery only make sense and are often only possible if they are understood as being pledged to an Absolute Thou. Thomas Anderson has described Marcel's identification of the unconditional nature of human relationships very well: "The other person is not seen as a person with a certain set of desirable characteristics, or as identified with a function, or even as a rational, autonomous subject; rather he or she is experienced as a 'thou,' a person with whom I identify and am one with on the path of life."[10] Clyde Pax has emphasized the religious dimension of such experiences when he points out that we often appeal to an ultimate strength which enables us to make a pledge of fidelity which we know we could not make from ourselves alone.[11] Human beings also have a reasonable hope in the ultimate intelligibility of existence. With regard to this ultimate hope, Marcel notes that, "The only possible source from which this absolute hope springs must once more be stressed. It appears as a response of the creature to the infinite Being to whom it is conscious of owing everything that it has and upon whom it cannot impose any condition whatsoever."[12] It is in this context that Marcel

---

9   Seymour Cain, *Gabriel Marcel* (South Bend, IN: Regnery, 1963), p. 87.

10 Thomas Anderson, "The Experiential Paths to God in Kierkegaard and Marcel," *Philosophy Today*, 26 (1982), p. 31.

11 See Clyde Pax, *An Existentialist Approach to God: A Study of Gabriel Marcel* (The Hague: Martinus Nijhoff, 1972), p.60.

12 Gabriel Marcel, *Homo Viator*, trans. by Emma Craufurd (Chicago: Regnery, 1952), p.47.

argues that it is no surprise that many human beings *experience* their lives as a gift; of course, a gift requires a *gift-giver*, an example of another indirect argument for the existence of a Supreme Being, one of several in his work.

Many of our most profound experiences, especially those that we find most challenging and that appeal to the very depths of our being, might also be understood to involve the notion of grace, a favor and helping hand from God in times of trial, the theme of one of the plays in the present volume. This point also complements his view that it is part of the essence of being human to feel a call to transcendence; this is part of our nature as human beings. One of the problems of modernity is that this call is being smothered because we live in what Marcel describes as a broken world. This is a world dominated by alienation, despair, and loss of meaning, but these are not the only responses to the finitude and freedom that characterize human existence.

III

This overview of Marcel's thought allows us to turn to his drama more directly, and to appreciate its philosophical significance. Drama provides another route of access to the realm of mystery. Marcel has reflected on the relationship between his dramatic work and his philosophical work in several places, and makes a number of interesting observations.[13] First, he notes that his dramatic work should be approached as a complement to his philosophical work. This is because one can reveal in dramatic art something of the realm of mystery that one is trying to explain in a more analytical, conceptual way in philosophy. There is a sense in which the audience of a play (or of a movie or musical performance) can enter into the work of art at what Marcel would call the existential level, at least to some degree, if the art is well crafted and performed. In drama especially one can recognize in the lives of the characters experiences and situations from one's own life, and also be led to reflect on them and to understand them with more clarity and depth. It is in this sense that great art captures something universal about the human condition.

---

13   See especially his full discussion in *The Existential Background of Human Dignity* (Cambridge, MA: Harvard University Press, 1963).

Second, Marcel notes that in some cases his dramatic creation antici-
pated his reflective thinking, rather than the other way around. This is particularly true in his treatment of the human experience of fidelity. It also
reminds us of a unique point about Marcel: the autobiographical nature of
much of his thought, and also his willingness, unlike many philosophers,
to reveal the struggle involved in working out his ideas, especially in his
early career. This is seen clearly in the fact that two of his early works are
written in a diary format, *Metaphysical Journal* (first published in 1927), and
Being and Having (1935) covering the period 1914–1933, when he was
wrestling with his main ideas in philosophy. The various entries in these
works range across the days and months of this time period, and provide a
rare glimpse of a philosopher in action as he engages with a number of
questions. Marcel here offers us an unusual insight into a philosopher at
work, a philosopher thinking out loud as it were, in the same way we might
watch a painter or a sculptor in action, and we should regard such an opportunity in a positive way rather than as a challenge. The editors of the
book series "The Library of Living Philosophers," in which each volume
contains an autobiographical essay as well as a number of articles on the
thought of the subject, note that Marcel's autobiographical reflections are
the most personal in the whole series.[14]

Third, Marcel tells us that he detests what he calls "philosophical
plays," plays where the characters are invented to illustrate philosophical
points, and notes tellingly that if his own plays were of this type, they would
add little to his philosophical writings, but in fact the reverse is true. The
dialogue method of drama does not seek to demonstrate points, but to reveal them in what Marcel describes as an "existential" manner, as the characters try to deal with situations that arise in their own experience,
situations that will also echo with the audience and reader. Fourth, he adds
that the plays deal with fundamental problems that arise in human relationships and in human experience, but that he deliberately does not try
to offer solutions. He presents the play as an opportunity for his audience
to reflect on their own lives and their own solutions.[15]

The two plays in the present volume were written very early in his

---

14   See Schilpp and Hahn (eds.), *The Philosophy of Gabriel Marcel*, p. xv.
15   See *The Existential Background of Human Dignity*, pp. 60–68.

career, and indeed are among his first publications. *La Grâce* (Grace) was written in 1910–11 and *La Palais de sable* (*The Sandcastle*) in 1913, and they were published together the following year under the title *Le Seuil invisible* (*The Invisible Threshold*). The first play, Grace, explores the theme of the nature of religious conversion and what it entails. Gerard's conversion allows for two different and irreconcilable interpretations. The first is the interpretation of the scientific materialist; the second regards Gerard's illness not as a cause but as an occasion to exercise the subject's creative freedom. The play also raises the question of grace: the role that God may play in the choice of faith. Marcel tells us that in this and many of his plays he does not take a position on the questions raised but leaves the reader to decide (although he holds a position, noting that he does not intend that both interpretations be regarded as equally valid, and points out that for one who has been touched by grace, it is impossible to accept a naturalistic interpretation[16]). Like most drama, the play presents scenarios that find their echo in our own experiences, that provoke us to work out our own responses and to discuss them with others. This approach to drama complements philosophy because the depiction of various life experiences helps us to "see" the true meaning in an existential, rather than a conceptual, manner; it may also provoke us to confront and to think through the questions raised in a more deliberative way than we ordinarily would. There is an interesting contrast between presenting a philosophical or a theological argument about the nature of grace, which includes an imaginary "concrete situation" in order to illustrate how grace might work in a specific case, and actually experiencing an occasion of grace in real life and how one might respond to it. This play attempts to depict real-life situations, as it were, and its two main protagonists, Frances and Gerard, come across as sincere even though they have diametrically opposed perspectives, as they struggle to make sense of their experiences, as we all must do.

Marcel tells us that the same themes are addressed but developed better in *The Sandcastle*. This play has a more intellectual side to it, as represented in the character of Moirans. The play raises the question of the confrontation between what one believes in an intellectual sense and the implications

---

16   See Gabriel Marcel, *Awakenings*, trans. P. Rogers (Milwaukee, IL: Marquette University Press, 2002) pp. 84–85.

and consequences of one's beliefs in real life. This is a profound theme, one that we all face as our beliefs and theories—especially about religion, morality, and politics—come up against situations in life that can test them. It raises issues of moral character, commitment, and sincerity, along with the matter of the logical consistency of one's beliefs. The play also introduces the role doubt can play in the way we form and hold our convictions. A number of very profound themes are raised and developed by Marcel, and there is an intensity throughout the dialogue as the characters struggle to understand their beliefs, motivations, and aims. The springboard for the unfolding of the drama is Moirans coming to realize the difference between accepting Christianity in an intellectual and cultural sense, and a Christianity that is lived. This theme then provokes his daughter, Clarisse (the only person in his family that Moirans respects, and in whom he sees something of himself), into some profound soul-searching of her own. There is also the theme of intersubjectivity where Moirans comes to the realization that self-consciousness and self-reflection may not be the way to truth and love.[17]

Marcel's drama offers audiences and readers a mirror that reflects their own problems, which can lead to further awareness and understanding. This complements his theme of secondary reflection where we go beyond ordinary reflection to appeal to our own experience to understand the nature of the human condition. What is the nature of this condition? According to Marcel, it is that there are profound human experiences such as love, fidelity, hope, and faith that are part of human nature, but that cannot be fully captured in conceptual knowledge. The plays deal especially with the difficulties in recognizing such experiences, in acknowledging them, in living them out in an authentic way, and often illustrate our failures with regard to them. Life's most profound and most fulfilling experiences are being compromised perhaps more than ever in our broken world, which is one of alienation, loss of meaning, and feelings of despair. These are the themes of his plays.

There is a sense in Marcel's plays, and throughout his work, particularly his later work, that if we were authentic Christians, making a strong effort

17 See Marcel's discussion of these two plays in *The Existential Background of Human Dignity*, pp. 28–34.

to live out Christian morality, not necessarily Christian dogma, it would solve many of our problems. More philosophically, this would also have to include a critique of philosophical atheism and materialism, along with a recognition of the transcendent realm and a consideration of the experience that life is a gift. I suspect that Marcel was reluctant to make these points so directly because of the influence of the philosophical milieu in which he worked. This is also one of the reasons he was reluctant to describe himself as a Christian existentialist, and did not like the fact that his work was often presented as a contrast to Sartre's (when it clearly is). In a sense his philosophy, as well as the two plays featured here, raise the question of the profound role that grace can play in human life, but do not draw out its full implications. At least in his plays, Marcel leaves that to us.

Brendan Sweetman,
Kansas City,
May 2018.

PREFACE

Gabriel Marcel

If I permit myself to precede this volume with a few words of explanation, it is less in the vain hope of imposing an interpretation on the reader than to summarily define the spirit in which I would like him to approach these dramas, the very spirit in which they were written. These dramas are essentially dramas of ideas, they move in the sphere of metaphysical thought, and yet they are not in any degree philosophical dialogues; they are concerned with the last contradictions that the mind uncovers in reflecting on itself, and yet we find there neither allegory nor symbol. I tried above all in these two plays to show the tragedy of thought realizing itself directly in the only state that deserves to be called life—that is, in consciousness.

The very idea of a tragic thought probably requires some clarification. Despite Ibsen and Curel, our contemporary authors continue for the most part to situate the tragic in a brutal game of wills or even more often of instincts that clash. And we must recognize that from these conflicts some form of tragedy can indeed be born. But this tragedy only addresses the nerves, the immediate sensibility; it only has command over us through a kind of suggestion that presents with real artistry rather distant connections. It is obvious that a completely different kind of tragedy is possible, in which the perception of great truths and great problems plays a decisive role.[18] It is not, as we see, a question of the tragic tearfulness of melodramatic thesis plays; we cannot condemn too much this contradictory and artificial genre which in fact involves a real legerdemain and too often

---

18   *The Freed* (*Les Affranchis*) of Miss Lenéru would partially illustrate this point. (A reference to a play by French Playwright, Marie Lenéru, 1875–1918, ed.)

portrays a rhetorical imagination. The emotion I am describing is similar to the one that great music gives. No offense to those for whom everything in music is reduced to a nervous commotion of sound, works such as Beethoven's last quartets move intellectually; they develop in us a superior life of thought that certainly cannot be translated discursively or explicitly in knowledge, but can be compared to the intimate fervor of a religious meditation.

And no doubt this superior musical emotion assumes an underpinning of feeling and of musical technique; in the same way the tragedy of thought can only occur in a certain affective atmosphere between characters of flesh and bone, living the same life as all of us, participating in the same weaknesses and the same passions. It could not live in the zone of abstraction, in the rarefied air of philosophical dialogue; it takes all its intensity from real life, among real people; and here, be it said in passing, is why it seems to me that several contemporary playwrights, Mr. Paul Claudel in the lead, despite his admirable gifts, are wrong in setting their works in non- realistic or indeterminate backgrounds. The ideal value of the drama, in my opinion, far from finding itself increased, is thereby reduced; the Idea is impoverished, until it becomes a pale abstraction.

The two plays that follow, therefore, take place in real settings quite similar to ours; the human examples are not heroes or exceptional beings; if they distinguish themselves from the average, it is in sum only by a sharper inner clairvoyance that allows them at times, not to analyze precisely, but to notice and to condense in an intuition, that which to a less penetrating mind, would remain in the dusty state of a disordered and elusive consciousness.

Convention, one will say!; not absolutely, because in present-day life, those who experience such tragedies are often distinguished by a singularly profound self-awareness. Furthermore, the theater, unless it be a literal reproduction without comfort, can only be an instrument of synthesis, that is to say it must illuminate by an intense glow the great sharp precipices of the soul beside which an ordinary observer could pass without suspecting anything. And undoubtedly we have witnessed in recent years a great effort to take advantage of the elements of tragedy related to the subconscious life of man; this lyricism of confused thinking, which originated in symbolism, has not failed to also invade the theater, and we owe to it some beautiful works.[19] But one may wonder if there does not lie therein a danger; only perhaps the genius of a Shakespeare or an Ibsen has the clarity of focus powerful enough to project light into the underground regions of the soul. A spirit of smaller breadth, in wanting to depict this indistinct world, risks falling into the arbitrary and vague, or contenting itself with poorly defined symbols and doubtful analogies. By its very nature, the order of the subconscious is the realm of interpretation and hypothesis; it can only be subject to individual and divergent readings; one explains in that way how it reveals itself to be rich in poetic material; the symbolic lyricism implies, as has been shown its recent exegetes, an infinite multiplicity of meanings variable according to the special faculties of the reader. In the theater, it is not absolutely so; certainly a tragedy should not be condensed into an absolute abstract formula that would exhaust its content; some lyrical elements, that is to say varied and individual themes can and must find a place there; but still it is necessary that they be subordinate to a certain external movement which is like the objective life of a drama. In other words it is imprudent to want to place the axis of the work in a subconscious process, only grasped by inference; the same principle which ensures the intelligibility of the drama then lies in a sort of beyond that dominates the actions and the words of the characters, and to which the reader or viewer must hoist himself by a special effort of divination. If he refuses to make this effort or is incapable of supplying it, these gestures and these words will appear to him absolutely arbitrary, and it will seem to him that he is floating in I don't know what intermundane space, halfway between abstraction and reality, between dream and life.

So I think that the drama must be explicit; the tragic lyricism that I want is a lyricism of clear consciousness. This lyricism would owe nothing to those emotions that one has exploited too much: uneasy surprise in the face of mystery, anguish before the unexpressed. They are in my view exhausted resources. Now it is a question of being courageous and no longer stopping like the frightened child who doesn't dare open wide the door left ajar; it's a question of approaching with a valiant look those prohibited spaces around which our contemporaries were pleased to prowl with anxiety

19 The influence of this lyricism in the work of Bataille is so obvious that it is not necessary to emphasize it.

and where they knew how to find delight: this attitude was legitimate as long as it was sincere; it is very clear that it has ceased to be so. The agnosticism of our elders makes us smile; we see little there but the laziness of stay-at-home intelligences that are frightened by the risks and surprises of travel. We have regained confidence in the value and the sovereign reality of the spirit, and a world that would jealously refuse the embrace of our thought would not seem worthy to us of our regrets; we can no longer situate the principle of all understanding in a region inaccessible to understanding; this unknowable before which we were invited to prostrate ourselves no longer appears to us as the mysterious source from which would emanate all thought, but as an indecisive zone where knowledge obscures itself in order to extinguish itself at last in the indeterminate.

Will one object that I am making the theater the instrument of a superficial and narrow ideology that claims to encompass the real within its inadequate concepts? This would very badly understand the attitude that I seek to define. The tragic in thought is not realized by the fixation in abstract symbols, by the concentration in cold rhetoric of the great spiritual conflicts; it can only emerge through the recreation of this evolution as it progresses. These conflicts are before expressing themselves, even justifying themselves logically; the clothing of the verb and the argumentation must cover no doubt the palpitating life of the drama, but in a way flexible enough that we feel the intimate thrill of it.

And without doubt the possibility or the value of such an esthetic cannot be easily proved any more than it can be refuted. Refutation and proof are empty of meaning in esthetics: these pages and the two dramas that follow are for those who before the great abyss of the interior life have felt the shiver of the infinite, to those for whom Ideas are not some abstract glimmers on the most despoiled summits of reflection, but penetrate to the marrow of life to infuse in it some eternal pathos. Outside of this, there is no room except for the incidental anecdote. In this sense I would really say that this book is for religious spirits and for them alone, for religion considered in its essence is not a neutral creed, bearing on transcendent realities, any more than it is a code of moral rules; it is faith in the absolute value of life, not in the deification of natural phenomenon, but in the assertion that there is only a true reality of the spirit, and that the rest is not important. This faith is the soul of this book; it is not a question of imparting it, because no matter what a certain mystic may say, it is by what is inferior in them that thoughts enter; but perhaps the reading of these dramas will facilitate in some way this union in one love and one anguish, outside of which there cannot be for a finite conscience any satisfaction or true rest.

(*1914*)

AN AGNOSTIC THINKS ABOUT GRACE: INTRODUCTION TO *GRACE*

Maria Traub

Gabriel Marcel grew up in a household which placed value on reason, culture, and moral principles but which was devoid of religious instruction of any kind. His father, a French government official and diplomat, was a lapsed Catholic and his mother, who was Jewish, died when he was four years old. His mother's sister and maternal grandmother doted on him, as did his father, who held agnostic views.

The desire to probe the meaning of existence and faith drew Marcel on a quest that eventually resulted in his conversion to Catholicism. In our first play, *Grace*, written before his conversion, Marcel places the main focus on two principal characters, Frances and Gerard, united to each other in marriage, but entirely opposed to each other in temperament, values, and understanding of spiritual matters

At the start of the play, we meet Frances, a young woman who fully supports independence and self-direction for women. She flaunts her scientific education and study of gynecology as proof that she understands a woman's physiology, and thus women; she has even written a play about an unconsummated marriage in which the rights and needs of the wife are at issue. While explaining her love for Gerard Launoy to her friend Antoinette, we learn that she has hidden her own authorship of this play from him. Gerard regards her as a pure young woman. He does not see how little she cares for spiritual matters nor how much sensual desire she really has. She does not notice his growing attraction to reflection and religious thought. She is primarily attracted to his good looks and his ability to charm women. Gerard, a poet, is a well-known young artist but longtime philanderer. His self-serving and easy morals do not make him a sound choice as a marriage partner. In addition Gerard has just learned that he has contracted tuberculosis. His past life and present condition weigh on him, so much that he seeks to cleanse his inner self. He sends Frances a telegram telling her that they must renounce each other. He wishes to cancel all plans but his fiancée will hear none of it. She convinces him that they should move ahead with their marriage as if nothing has happened. In spite of circumstances the couple marries in the first act, thus following the convictions of Frances. She even keeps Gerard's illness a secret from her family before they are married. Their marriage from the start is inauthentic. It is not built on a solid foundation of mutual sincerity but upon the insistence, strong-armed persuasion, and secrecy of one of the partners,

Frances, a student in psychopathology, has been working for Dr. Du Ryer, who is infatuated with her. They both share the same views which essentially reflect belief only in what can be proven scientifically. Frances is depicted as a strong-willed young woman, who dismisses the traditions and beliefs of her parents, and affirms a new modern direction. Early in the play, in a conversation with Mme. Letellier, a friend of her mother's, she states: "Well no, dear, Madam. You must take us as we are. We are women. We know life. We are no longer the nice little trinkets that you were, you others, forty years ago."

Frances shares her outlook with Mme. Letellier while discussing a play that Madame has recently been to see, the very play written by Frances whose intrigue is about a husband who could not fulfill his marital duties! The central question debated in this drama is: "Does the wife have the right to take a lover?" Mme. Letellier regards the play as scandalous. Frances's view is that, "Love is a force of nature." Frances has written the play under a pen-name, a fact she has concealed from most people, including her family and Mme. Letellier. Later in the first act of *Grace*, after Frances receives the telegram from Gerard, she exclaims: "But this cannot be, my happiness must not escape me like this." Thinking aloud, she says to herself: "Only one thing matters, it is death. He could disappear without my having been his." For Frances, self-centeredness, haste, and emphasis on material things are foremost in her decision-making.

In Marcel's play, it is apparent that for Frances, sexual union with Gerard is a primary reason to marry him. To possess and be possessed by him is her fondest wish. We never read that the two have discussed or shared their ideas, values, plans about the future, or forged unbreakable ties. While Frances is longing for a physical relationship with him, Gerard has undergone a spiritual awakening. His response to it changes his life; it is a response to grace, to an intangible entity, a call to draw closer to God.

For clarity about the issue of grace, and the soul's response to it, we might consider some simple definitions. Grace as defined in the *Catechism* of the Catholic Church is "favor, the free and undeserved help that God gives to us to respond to his call to become children of God, adoptive sons, partakers of the divine nature and of eternal life." There are two kinds of grace: actual and sanctifying. Actual grace resembles a supernatural push or encouragement; it is transient, it does not live in the soul but acts on the soul. It is a supernatural "wake-up call," a push in the right direction, so to speak. It is a gift to the will and the intellect. For example, if one becomes repentant, one is probably responding to a grace from God to atone for one's sins. Actual grace acts on the soul from the outside and gets it moving in the right direction—if the soul chooses to respond to it. It gets the will and intellect moving to seek out and keep sanctifying grace, which keeps the soul healthy and holy. Sanctifying grace is grace that stays in the soul, and makes the soul holy. It gives supernatural life to the soul. If the soul deliberately chooses evil, sanctifying grace disappears. Sanctifying grace leads the soul to purification, and in order to be in perfect and absolute union with God, the source of all life, we need souls that are pure and good. Souls besmirched with mortal and deadly sins cannot coexist with God because sin kills off the spiritual life, the sanctifying grace.

As Frances sees it, the effect of grace in Gerard's life is disastrous. She views it as no more than a fatal whim that is pulling him away from her. In Act Two, she states, "Grace will soon have completed its work of destruction. All that I have loved, all that I have desired, all will be torn from me." Frances resents the so-called action of grace in Gerard's life. Her hope to have a marriage to Gerard who will be as a "lover" to her is shattered. Nursing an invalid was something she was prepared to do from the start, but only for a husband who would heal and become her passionate spouse. The shock of seeing her sickly beloved's heart intently drawn toward the spiritual and away from her causes her to become embittered.

This play is a look inside the lives of a couple who are at different stages along an inner journey, moving toward or away from the lifelines of grace.

Each is seeking an understanding: Frances wishes to draw Gerard closer to her; Gerard wishes to learn more about faith. They are groping about, testing and searching for truth. Gerard's detachment and unresponsive behavior to Frances frustrates and disappoints her.

Hilda Lazaron writes of Marcel as a playwright, that, "Male characters often suffer from insufficient power to act and are consequently unable to find satisfaction in their goals; in contrast with the women, always strong, whose strength often defeats their opportunity for happiness."[20] Gerard, believing that Frances was dedicated to the good work of nursing him, passively goes along with her. As time progresses, she becomes more and more dissatisfied with her marriage. For Gerard, who, with the fervor of a fresh convert, turns more and more to his faith, the focus on the physical side of a marital relationship becomes secondary.

Essentially, the protagonists are mistaken from the start because they understand each other quite differently and are pursuing different goals. Gerard believed Frances to be a very chaste young woman, who through pure love for him wished to nurse him back to health. Gerard's understanding considered Frances a partner who shared his ideals. Frances simply wanted his attention, his approval, and most of all, his passionate love. After she is married and faces the reality of it all she observes:

> What he loves in me is a chaste and fearful stranger that I do not know; I trembled on the day that for the first time I understood what strange image he had of me and loved instead of me. And then, moved by I don't know what irresistible force, I began to apply myself with all my might to resemble this false image. Do you understand now my pain? Do you understand what it is for me to be obliged to lie to myself, and to lie to the one that I love more than myself, when sincerity is the only duty that I have ever understood, the only one that I have ever practiced?

It is a terribly sad situation that both young people are attracted to one another and love each other, even if differently, but have complete misunderstanding

20 Lazaron, Hilda, *Gabriel Marcel the Dramatist* (Gerrards Cross, UK: Colin Smythe Ltd., 1978), p. 31.

of one another. The experience of illness causes Gerard to become attentive mainly to the spiritual. An illness, particularly a serious one, may cause such a reaction in a soul. It may in some cases cause it to be responsive to grace. Frances notes the gradual development of mysticism in Gerard. While she can only accept the scientific and the proven, his attraction to the spiritual order is frustrating to her desire for his attention. Her desire as a married woman for the fullness of married life and love is natural. Gerard's only wish, however, is to deepen his faith, to contemplate life and death. His desires are far from the sensual order. The issues, desires, and non-negotiables of each of them force them apart. They cannot communicate with each other, they are locked into their own thinking. Frances is lonely and unfulfilled; Gerard is absorbed in the spiritual and in exile from the world.

While visiting Montana for new treatment options and for its healthy environment, Gerard's health improves. Frances receives an unusual and somewhat suspect visit from Dr. Du Ryer and his wife. It is during this visit that Frances betrays Gerard with her former professor and mentor. The liaison endures for the duration of Du Ryer's visit. In the last act the couple have returned to Paris but are preparing to depart again for a stay in the south. Gerard's condition has improved but his heart "gave the doctor some concern," as he reveals in a conversation with Oliver, Frances's brother. Thanks to a heated exchange with Frances earlier in the act, Gerard now understands her unfulfilled desire. Her loneliness and her desperate passion have moved him and rekindled his desire for physical love. In an attempt to make amends, he wishes to share an intimate evening with her alone. That same evening, Frances receives a visit from her close friend, Antoinette, who is in an "arranged marriage." During the visit, Antoinette innocently remarks that she would never cheat on her husband. This statement somehow causes Frances to feel the guilt and burden of her infidelity. She is visibly upset.

Gerard longs to share time alone with his wife. As he attempts to draw closer to her, she confesses to Gerard her transgression with Du Ryer. The shock of her statements affects not only his spirit but also his heart. He collapses and dies in her arms after telling God that everything has happened as he [God] had wished. Oliver had entered the room after Gerard's collapse. Upon looking closely at the dying Gerard and listening to his faint remarks, he experiences a deepening of his own faith. Thus, the example of Gerard's response to grace has moved Oliver and kindled his faith.

The play raises philosophical questions about marriage and the response to grace. In the first act, mention is made of a play whose true author has used a pseudonym. It is the play written by Frances. In a singular way, the intrigue of this play provides a prequel for what follows. It favors extramarital relationships for partners in marriage in which one of them is unable to perform the marital act. This prequel gives us a forecast of the actual story line to follow. There is a mirroring effect present in several other places. Gerard's encounter with Father Andre in Montana places him before a priest who was formerly married but who renounced marriage to enter the priesthood. It is in conversation with him that Gerard predicts his death, which would also provide an end to his marriage.

Marcel does not debate the question of grace in a theological sense. The types of grace and the teachings about it are not at issue in the play. We have no analyses or long reflections upon spiritual teachings. Grace is seemingly at work in its mysterious way in real-life situations. It is ultimately considered and accepted by some as its effects are critiqued by others, which reflects Marcel's dramatic approach—to present various scenarios for us to think about.

The play's primary characters may be Frances and Gerard but Oliver, her brother, is a character who experiences a turning point. In Act Two, Oliver is anxious and admits lack of a strong faith but during the closing lines of the play he is impressed by Gerard's spiritual commitment: "... The strength of belief is surely the measure of being ... Your faith is as real to my eyes as dreams and as life ...." As Frances throws herself, sobbing, over the inanimate body of Gerard, Oliver muses: "Nothing more than a look ... And now, on the strength of that look ..."

Marcel's point is that faith and grace are real, invisible yet salient forces in man's being. The gifts are free as are their acceptance and use—this freedom is yet another gift.

GRACE
(*La Grâce*)
BY GABRIEL MARCEL
A PLAY IN FIVE ACTS

TRANSLATED FROM THE FRENCH BY MARIA TRAUB

CAST OF CHARACTERS

Gerard Launoy, 28 years old

Philip Du Ryer, 40 years old

Oliver Thouret, 19 years old

Charles Morin, 27 years old

Father Andre, 50 years old

Frances, 24 years old

Mrs. Thouret, 52 years old

Antoinette Raymond, 24 years old

Lucy Gauvin, 28 years old

Mrs. Letellier, 55 years old

Marianne Du Ryer, 30 years old

A housekeeper

ACT ONE

A living room in the home of Mrs. Thouret, in the background a door leading to the foyer; to the right a door which gives access to a large salon; to the left a window through which one glimpses the maze of rooftops of the Trocadero.

Act One: Scene One

Mrs. Thouret, Mrs. Letellier, then Frances

(At the start of the scene, one hears Frances who is singing the ending measures of "La Chevelure" by Debussy, in a room off to the side. The Art song is sung in French.)

FRANCES: "Il mit doucement la main sur mon épaule et il me regarda d'un regard si tendre que je baissais les yeux avec un frisson ..."

[He gently placed his hand upon my shoulder and he looked at me with a look so tender that I lowered my eyes with a shiver ...]

MRS. LETELLIER: Did you see the subject of the new play at the Escholiers? They don't know what to invent anymore; but this time they are beyond belief. And they affirm *(ironically)* that the author is a woman of the world!

MRS. THOURET: No, what is it about? I am no longer able to read the paper, with the visits, the charity sales, and bridge ... But Frances was there with her sister and her brother-in-law *(face of Mrs. Letellier is serious and exhibits negativity and some distress)*. What? Is it that bad?

MRS. LETELLIER: But, my friend, it's quite simply regarded as the most shocking and the most disgusting since ... since several weeks ago.

MRS. THOURET: *(resigned)* Ah? I didn't know ... Besides, as soon as I am able to open my mouth, my son-in-law makes fun of me. So I no longer say anything.

MRS. LETELLIER: (*volubly*) It's quite simply the story of a man who can no longer fulfill his conjugal duties. The wife, does she have the right to take a lover? That is the question that one debates throughout four acts.

FRANCES: (*coming in and overhearing*) You are forgetting to say that the woman does not want to divorce because of the child.

MRS. LETELLIER: (*sardonically*) She's a good mother?

FRANCES: (*facing her*) Why not? What is there contradictory about that?

MRS. THOURET: Frances, my child ...

FRANCES: Please explain to me, dear madam, why it scandalizes you so much that I would have gone to see this play?

MRS. LETELLIER: No, no, I am not saying anything anymore ... I am not meddling into what does not concern me ...

FRANCES: Explain to me, just to make me happy. Come now, do you believe I don't know about such things, do you think so?

MRS. LETELLIER: I do not believe anything ... all I know, my dear child, is that it would be better, and for everyone, if young ladies were a little less informed.

FRANCES: Mrs. Letellier, Mrs. Letellier, let's see ... I took a course at the university on gynecology, and you wish that the physical dimensions of marriage, of love ...

MRS. LETELLIER: That has nothing to do with love.

FRANCES: (*with irony*) Ah? (*a silence*)

MRS. LETELLIER: And then no one says that all this intellectual culture is good for the health of young girls. (*to Mrs. Thouret*) The daughter of my friend Altberger is once again bedridden...For the second time this winter ...

FRANCES: Allow me to say that you are diverting the issue, the fact is, I took a course ...

MRS. THOURET: Come now, Frances, my child ...

FRANCES: Mama, allow Mrs. Letellier to explain herself.

MRS. LETELLIER: Well! I find that it's not a good reason that just because you know things, you should go listen to such horrors in a theater. The world ...

FRANCES: I expected the world. So you find it fine, you do, this hypocrisy, this false ingenuity! We have left our daughter at home, they say, it's a little too steep for her. And during this time the innocent young girl is reading the play in *The Illustration*. Yes, but she is not exposed to indiscreet glances; one is not spying on her to see if she is offended, if she is shocked. Well, dear madam, it is all the same to me that one spies upon me, because I know that one will not see anything, and that for this good reason, I am not shocked.

MRS. LETELLIER: So then, this situation does not shock you?

FRANCES: (*provocatively*) What is there that is shocking? The only fault of the author is to not have been sufficiently precise (*gesture of shock on the part of Mrs. Letellier*); the causes of the husband's condition are not determined.

MRS. LETELLIER: My child, you shock me, you speak of these things with such ease, such aplomb ... It's madness, it's mad ... When I think back to our days as young women; you do remember, dear Madame, don't you?

MRS. THOURET: Oh! Me, they only permitted me to see *Phèdre* eight days before my marriage ...

MRS. LETELLIER: I assure you, Frances, for your own interests ... That it is wrong.

FRANCES: That's all fine, preserve the appearances of ignorance and of simplicity, when one is neither ignorant nor naive. To be innocent, to blush on call ... Eh, well no, dear Madame. One must take us as we are. We are women, we understand life, we are happily no longer the nice little trinkets that you were, you others, forty years ago. For the poet, for the bad poet to decry our lost innocence. You used to find it quite all right, all of you, the young girl who knew nothing the evening before and who knew everything the day after? You find it reasonable and agreeable, the brusque initiation into the sacred mysteries (*the two women look at each other with consternation*), and you also believe that it is thus that one produces honest women?

MRS. LETELLIER: Here I am stopping you, look around you: your mother, your aunt ...

FRANCES: I know, I know; but there are all the others, all those who discovered love too late, all those who have been placed too late in front of life ...

MRS. THOURET: You are exciting yourself, you are exciting yourself, you would do much better to return to your piano.

FRANCES: Yes, you are right, Mama ... goodbye, dear Madame, and excuse me (*she leaves*).

Act One: Scene Two

Mrs. Thouret, Mrs. Letellier

MRS. THOURET: My dear friend, I am confused. I hope that this child has not hurt you (*gesture of denial by Mrs. Letellier*) I assure you that I'm tired of these responsibilities ...

MRS. LETELLIER: Permit me to say that they do not seem to weigh upon you too much ...

MRS. THOURET: But what do you want me to do? Can I stop her from starting her medical studies, and from reading what she wishes and from taking courses of psychophysiology and from going to the laboratory? Could I take offense at seeing my daughter intelligent, curious, and desiring to learn? Would you rather that she remain constantly with an unknowledgeable mama like me? One must resign oneself; the times have changed, my dear. We accepted life as it was presented to us. Today, they wish to know, to understand, and to criticize. Perhaps all of that will seem natural in twenty years ... But all the same I am not angry that she is getting married.

MRS. LETELLIER: Is the date decided?

MRS. THOURET: Of course, it's the fifteenth, didn't you know? You must absolutely make the acquaintance of Frances's fiancé beforehand.

MRS. LETELLIER: I have already met Mr. Launoy several times.

MRS. THOURET: Isn't he charming? My daughter made his acquaintance at the home of some friends. And I admit that Gerard won my approval from the first moment that I saw him.

MRS. LETELLIER: He seemed to me to be very charming, exceptionally distinguished overall, and in addition to that, he did not have that horrible American way about him that so many young people try to adopt these days.

MRS. THOURET: He is simplicity itself, but what I especially like about him is an astonishing delicacy of feeling. Did you know that he was raised by his mother and that he always lived with her, right up to the end? The poor woman died but two years ago.

MRS. LETELLIER: That explains the inexplicable refinement he has in his movements, and the almost feminine softness of his gaze.

MRS. THOURET: (*dreamily*) Feminine, yes (*a silence*). He already knows all my tastes, all my quirks, just imagine, he knows them better than Frances.

MRS. LETELLIER: But what exactly is his position?

MRS. THOURET: He writes; I have here a volume of poetry by him ...
He never prepared any special career; he was infatuated by many things in
succession; at one time archeology tempted him, and then he gave up on
it. He is an exquisite boy. I am very, (*insistent*) very happy.

Act One: Scene Three

The same characters; Philip Du Ryer, then Charles Morin

MRS. THOURET: (*to Du Ryer*) How kind it is of you to come! Frances is
going to be so happy; is Mrs. Du Ryer doing well? Dear friend, allow me
to introduce you to Mr. Du Ryer, of whom you no doubt have heard mention. Frances was his pupil.

DU RYER: A pupil of whom I am proud.

MRS. THOURET: I think that she has been reading your work on the
Psychology of the Apostles for a while—she has not yet had the time to finish
it.

DU RYER: Miss Thouret must be very busy at this time; I fear that I am
disturbing her.

MRS. THOURET: Not at all, not at all, it will give her the greatest pleasure.

MRS. LETELLIER: Dear friend, I must take my leave. A conference at
the Annals ... Sir ...

MRS. THOURET: I'll accompany you ... (*to Du Ryer*) You will excuse
me; I am going to send Frances in to you.

(*Du Ryer leafs through his book with complacency, Frances enters.*)

FRANCES: Mr. Du Ryer! Well! That makes me happy. And so: what is new?

DU RYER: Nothing; we miss you (*ironic smile of Frances*). You don't believe me? You are free to ... Tell me, will we not be seeing you at the Laboratory?

FRANCES: You would not wish it. All that has basically been a pastime, a pastime of an idle young lady. What would you like me to do in Saint-Anne's now? And I think that it would not please my fiancé very much.

DU RYER: Mr. Launoy is not very interested in science?

FRANCES: I am afraid that he hardly cares about it. And you see, I am not bothered by it; because for me too it seems that I have never taken science seriously. I did the laboratory work as others play in a comedy.

DU RYER: I recall however the passionate attention with which you followed our sick ones, Amelia for example.

FRANCES: Yes, it amused me; and I am one of those who pursue their whims in totality and who treat them as obligations; as a child I'd apply myself to a game as to an obligation; that does not mean anything. What for you is the very interest in life has only ever been for me but a diversion.

DU RYER: I think you are fooling yourself about what you used to think.

FRANCES: No, I assure you. Besides, what does it matter? A student, a novice, more or less ...

DU RYER: Ah! Don't say that. Only I can know what a valuable recruit you would have been for our scientific work; I who have seen your mind at work. I have been able to observe that rigorous logic in deductions, that impartiality in observation, and then above all that willpower not to let oneself be duped by words, to find the true and profound cause. You remember Henriette, that visionary, that mystic. You are the one who suggested the possibility of an explanation due to a heart condition. So many other women would have ...

FRANCES: I know. I know. What does all that matter? (*Smiling*) All of it! If my brother heard you, I believe he would pour insults on us both. We would hear a thing or two about science and about psychology.

DU RYER: He is still very young. Why doesn't he study his medicine? It would be good for him, I assure you. Instead of straying into chimeras and into words ...

FRANCES: (*cutting him short*) All the same I myself feel a real satisfaction to think I will no longer see those women that you were talking about just now. With those madwomen nearby, I often shivered thinking of what it would take to make us like them.

DU RYER: (*seriously*) Mental health is a perpetual miracle; besides, in the strictest sense there are no sane people.

FRANCES: (*pensively*) That philosophy renders one indulgent.

DU RYER: (*a little pedantically*) Indulgence is a word devoid of scientific signification. (*Enter Charles Morin*)

FRANCES: Charles (*to Du Ryer*) You surely know Mr. Morin, perhaps you have even read his book on Fra Angelico? (*Turning toward Charles*) It is kind of you to have come.

CHARLES: Don't be afraid; when you are married you will not see me often ... yes, yes, I know what I'm talking about. (*Turning toward Du Ryer*) There you are, sir, the man of the hour. Is it true that you are going to do a conference about the Apostles with projected images? ... You are knitting your brows. I am not kidding. Can't one reproduce the Durer of Munich if one wishes? Believe me, I admire your book a great deal. You seem to have said new and essential things about the liver of Saint Paul. I have always loved naturalist novels.

FRANCES: Let's speak of other things, say (*we hear the telephone ringing*). If you will excuse me I must get the telephone (*she leaves*).

DU RYER: (*following her with his eyes*) What a loss for psychology! True intelligence is so rare among women. And what charm withal!

CHARLES: Yes, she is perfect, on condition not to marry her. Will you permit me a question right now, Mr. Du Ryer, an indiscreet question, I fear. By admitting first that this can be established, and second that it is, what does it mean for us that Saint Paul might have had a liver crisis before arriving in Damascus?

DU RYER: (*stunned*) What, but it is what explains …

CHARLES: (*interrupting him*) So, therefore, we do not understand the same thing by the explanation. Rather, I claim that it explains nothing. Let's admit the facts; you say that hepatitis is the cause of the conversion of Saint Paul, very well, but if it pleases me to say that it was the instrument (*gesture of Du Ryer*). Ah! You find that it is a question of words? The hepatic crisis could very well be one of the ways that infinite wisdom used to bring about an event essential to the spiritual life of the Universe.[21] Why couldn't nature lead one to grace? What do you answer?

DU RYER: (*smiling*) Nothing, I respond nothing, Sir. I am not a psychologist and only know the facts. Experimental science …

CHARLES: Let's talk about it, about experimental science which claims to reconstruct the physiological state of those who were living two thousand years ago, while it has no … (*pressing the point*) no documents; about experimental science which works on the unknown and the unknowable and bases itself on assumptions, without understanding their scope. Experimental science! Yes, truly experimental, because it permits us, we who are of simple faith, like that of children, and who like children marvel at the riches of the world and of its beauty …

21 Capitalization is Marcel's.

DU RYER: (*interrupting*) Pardon, I ...

CHARLES: I beg your pardon ... It permits us to measure the unfathomable pride of one who while infinitely extending his incomprehension, believes that the world is as vain as he is, and only sees an immense and useless gear which would work in a vacuum, like his brain!

DU RYER: But what is the meaning of? ...

FRANCES: (*returning*) Just imagine. Antoinette returned just yesterday from Egypt and was calling to ask if I was at home. Well, what's wrong? Why this upset face?

DU RYER: The gentleman did me the honor of taking me apart over my interpretation of the conversion of Saint Paul.

CHARLES: You do not interpret it, you deny it.

FRANCES: My God, what importance does all of that have? If you only knew how little these things matter to me now. I am only thinking of the nice cup of tea that all of us will have together. Well, Charles, you are getting up? Come now, be reasonable. What can all that do? It's such an old story the conversion of Saint Paul.

CHARLES: (*somberly*) Look here, I much prefer the doctoral fanaticism of the gentleman than this indifference, this tolerance, which is only spinelessness. Go on, when these questions cease to arouse interest, it's a sign that a Society[22] is dying. What that can do ... On the one hand, I know the doctrine of over-educated hypochondriacs who keep us enslaved to our bodies because they themselves digest badly, on the other hand ... Ah! You don't deserve to know.

FRANCES: (*amused*) Tell us.

CHARLES: No. (*With irony*) What difference does it make? (*In a different*

22 Capitalization is Marcel's.

tone) But beware. Spiritual forces make their way around the world, whatever you make of it; they are at work, and they laugh at your indulgence, your tolerance, your indifference. The duel between nature and grace is not ended; when the hour of reconciliation will come this world will be ready to disappear. Beware. Fear the revenge of the spirit that you disregard.

FRANCES: (*crossing her arms*) Ah! As for that my friend, where do you think you are? What is this tone of a Hebrew prophet? You have not accustomed me to these outbursts. What does this mean? What is nature and what is grace?

CHARLES: Perhaps you will know it someday. (*To Du Ryer*) I am sure that you will find an explanation for this inexplicable violence. I am even able to furnish it for you. I ate American lobster last night.

(*He leaves.*)

Act One: Scene Four

Frances, Du Ryer, Antoinette

DU RYER: It's very curious; this tone of prophecy ... it's a very singular case.

FRANCES: I don't know what has gotten into him. The love of paradox, I suppose, but it is not intellectual.

Enter Antoinette Raymond.

FRANCES: There you are, my dear!

ANTOINETTE: I hurried into a taxi and here I am. Sir ...

FRANCES: You know each other; Mr. Du Ryer, my friend Antoinette Raymond.

DU RYER: I am forced to say farewell (*he rises*).

FRANCES: Thank you for your kind visit, and pardon for the simpleton Charles Morin (*she accompanies him to the door*).

Act One: Scene Five

Antoinette, Frances

FRANCES: Well my dear! Let's kiss first, eh! There you are all tanned by the sun ... You'll tell me all about it later: the mornings on the Nile, Philae, the sunset over the Pyramids ... Oh! Your letters! It seemed to me that I was stocking supplies of sunlight.

ANTOINETTE: But you, my dear, you! To think that I haven't seen you since you got engaged (*looking at her attentively*). Now I think that you are happy.

FRANCES: Happy! ... Oh! It is something else, better than happiness. Happiness is quite dry, it's how stupid it seems to me; if it was just happiness I think that I would not be happy. It's something else, it's ... You'll see him shortly, he will be coming.

ANTOINETTE: But tell me everything; your letters have told me nothing.

FRANCES: I can tell you nothing. You will see him and that will have to suffice for you to understand. The words that I would use to tell you what I feel do not communicate anything of this plenitude ... What would I say to you? That he is handsome? I don't know what ridiculous image, I know not what Anglo-Saxon Apollo would arise before your eyes, and that's not it. It's not therefore that he is handsome; he is handsome because I love him, and I love him ... because I am me. And that isn't it either. He activates a thousand aspirations of which I was unaware and which find expression now that they are satisfied.

ANTOINETTE: And you loved him from the start?

FRANCES: I no longer remember. I think my heart did not fumble ... I met him at the Aubertins' ... But there is a detail that you are unaware of; I don't know why, I preferred not to say it. What triggered my curiosity was the presence at the soirée of Mrs. Chauvé with whom I knew that he had broken up; I spied on him; it's bizarre, isn't it? It's thus that I paid attention to him. But what does all that matter; I have started to live since.

ANTOINETTE: (*pensive*) It's strange ...

FRANCES: What is it?

ANTOINETTE: Nothing; I recall that October evening when you came to see me to confide your distress, your passion for another—one who never knew of it. I was still thinking about it a short while ago on seeing both of you together. All the same, who would suspect the place he held in your dreams!

FRANCES: You cannot know how unreal this past passion seems to me now ... When I see this professorial and almost naively candid face of a man who has never lived, and I remember my ... How could he have not noticed? It is perhaps this very candor that was attracting me!

ANTOINETTE: You were saying to me: never will I love my husband as I love this man.—Oh! These evolutions of the heart! ... You'll tell your fiancé this story? Will you tell him about it?

FRANCES: He will know everything: I don't want to have secrets from him whom I love; and besides, would he be able to believe that my heart and my senses have never spoken? Tell me, would he? What ingénue would be able to create a similar illusion? And then, what does it matter. I love for the first time.

ANTOINETTE: Like all the others—all the other times ... My dear one! It seems to me that I would prefer not to see him, your fiancé. You love him, that is enough. If I don't like him, what will I say to you? He will perhaps strike me as an ordinary man, and when you'll look at me with shining eyes, what will I say to you?

FRANCES: Ah! Be quiet, you are talking about him as of a painting that one is going to see for the first time, you are talking about him as of a dead thing which may please or not. He is my life, Antoinette. I love him like a lover, do you understand? ... Do you remember?

ANTOINETTE: Yes, you were saying to me: if I do not love my husband like a lover, I am not able to remain an honest woman.

FRANCES: And these things, you were the only one to whom I could say them, because you, you understood. And somehow, you, you have never experienced all of that.

ANTOINETTE: No, never.

FRANCES: Your life will be strangely different from mine, since the one who is destined for you ...

ANTOINETTE: The one that I have accepted.

FRANCES: ... That has never made your heart beat faster.

ANTOINETTE: It is true ...

FRANCES: And yet when he returns in six months, you'll be ready to leave with him for lost countries, for this dull life side by side?

ANTOINETTE: Yes; but what good is there to talk about it? That's the way it is. I will always remain an outsider to your joys and anguish, and yet somehow I understand. I understand, but I do not feel as you do. Love— that love ...

FRANCES: You can speak of love, go on, my poor dear.

ANTOINETTE: Love will remain for me the drama that is played out on the stage, and I will only ever be a curious spectator ... Let's talk about something else, shall we? Well! How about your play?

FRANCES: (*lowering her voice*) It was performed, did you see it? And a real success.

ANTOINETTE: But no one knows that it is by you?

FRANCES: No. Lucy and her husband only, who took me to see it; and our cousin Henry who directed all the rehearsals.

ANTOINETTE: And your fiancé, naturally.

FRANCES: No, not even ... Not yet ... Can you imagine I was too cowardly to tell him about it. Well, I'll tell him shortly when he arrives.

ANTOINETTE: But why hide it from him?

FRANCES: I don't know ... or rather ... Listen Antoinette, you see, we are all cowards, even the bravest. I feared, I don't know why, that it might be unpleasant for him.

ANTOINETTE: Would he be shocked so easily?

FRANCES: You are crazy. After all, I preferred to wait.

ANTOINETTE: Curious ... In short, what is your conclusion? You admit the right of a woman to take a lover?

Act One: Scene Six

The same characters; Oliver

OLIVER: What! You are back? But I didn't know. Oh! But I'm interrupting an animated conversation. Naturally, I only heard the word lover; what was it about? (*Frances seems a bit embarrassed.*)

ANTOINETTE: We were talking about the play at Escholiers.

OLIVER: That ignominy? Never has the materialism of love been so far off. How can you talk about that? As for me, I find that that dirties the imagination.

ANTOINETTE: (*to Frances laughing*) Your brother pulls no punches.

OLIVER: No, but seriously, what interest can you find in a subject like that one which rests entirely on an illness? And then it's as if a woman ceased to owe fidelity to her husband because ...

ANTOINETTE: Keep going.

OLIVER: No; I shouldn't speak about that with you.

FRANCES: He wants to say that it is shocking.

ANTOINETTE: Ah! That's it? You are funny, Oliver. What difference does it make?

FRANCES: If you start a discussion with Oliver, you never finish.

ANTOINETTE: It seems to me that you have become very intransigent, Oliver.

FRANCES: Become? He has always been like that. For two years I was not able to read my lines because they were offensive to him.

ANTOINETTE: (*amused*) That's true? (*Oliver blushes.*) But what importance has all that? I find that it gives honor to love, basically, to be offended so easily. When one thinks about what it actually is ...

OLIVER: (*violently*) By what you have done, you and your friends and all those horrible young people who no longer know how to distinguish between the most brutal passion and true love, deep love ...

ANTOINETTE: Oliver, you impress me.

OLIVER: These creatures without thought and without ideals who have soiled everything and who after that are bringing over to the worst scoundrels indulgences which they themselves enjoy unduly, have begun to rehabilitate the prostitute and to be moved to tears by the pimp!

ANTOINETTE: Oliver, you are getting carried away, beware ... will you take things calmly?

OLIVER: Yes, yes, you can laugh; all that is true nevertheless; and it's because this sickness of the present age is contagious that you are making fun of me; you do not suffer from that humiliation into which a society has fallen which believed itself tolerant, while in fact it was only an accomplice.

FRANCES: The second time today that I am hearing a prophet ...

ANTOINETTE: Oliver, the priest at Saint-Augustine is waiting for you; go, go quickly to confess yourself, you must shorten your time in purgatory.

FRANCES: You want to joke, but Oliver has often told me that later he would return to the faith of our fathers. Meanwhile he will attend mass every Sunday. He only reads René Bazin, Henri Bordeaux, and Paul Bourget,[23] the later volumes, the first ones are too perverse.

ANTOINETTE: It's fantastic.—I thought he was a socialist, like everyone else.

OLIVER: (*sarcastically*) You are a socialist?

ANTOINETTE: Oh! Me, you know, politics ...

OLIVER: Obviously you prefer stories of the alcove like Frances (*pressing*), matters of sophistic intimacy, as in the play.

ANTOINETTE: (*thoughtlessly*) Oh! Let Frances's play alone!

OLIVER: (*astonished*) Frances's play?

23 Catholic authors of this period.

FRANCES: Yes, the play that I went to see.

OLIVER: (*a little pensive*) The play that she went to see ...

ANTOINETTE: (*awkwardly changing the conversation*) Then you like that, this machine Bazin? ...

OLIVER: (*interrupting her*) You have quite a hurried air to speak about something else. (*He looks at Frances who diverts her eyes a little.*) Come, come, it's not possible ... Frances's play. In fact, she was nervous the other night. (*With a shout.*) Frances, this thing is yours! How could you! ...

FRANCES: But, my darling, you're crazy. It's signed Jules Dupont.

OLIVER: It's stupid. It's a pseudonym.

FRANCES: A pseudonym? Does it sound like a pseudonym?

OLIVER: The first duty of a pseudonym ... And then if it wasn't true you would not discuss it.

FRANCES: (*nervously*) My boy, I inform you that you ...

Act One: Scene Seven

The same characters; Lucy Gauvin

OLIVER: We shall see ... Lucy, what do you think of Frances's play?

LUCY: What, do you know then ...

OLIVER: This time you'll no longer deny it! ... But how could you? ... (*He bursts into tears.*)

LUCY: What is the matter?

FRANCES: Oliver, you are crazy.

OLIVER: (*In tears*) No, this passes the limit. An obscene subject ... You! ... Mama will know ...

FRANCES: Oliver, I forbid you to tell Mama about it; you understand.

OLIVER: You forbid me; and by what right?

LUCY: You would give her palpitations, dear one. My God, what an affair! And I came here to rest after my errands!

OLIVER: Mama will know it.

ANTOINETTE: What a child! (*To Frances*) He will not do it.

FRANCES: Oh! You don't know him; he has always been a tattletale. (*Antoinette roars with laughter.*)

LUCY: And I'm starving ... (*to Antoinette*) so come with me into the dining room; we'll surely find something. It is better to leave them alone.

Act One: Scene Eight

Oliver, Frances

FRANCES: See here, darling, be reasonable, what can all of that do? How can one put oneself into such a state over so little? And your New Youth dinner just now! You will not be presentable. Child, go on child!

OLIVER: (*lugubriously*) It had to happen ...

FRANCES: Hush! Hush! It's a phrase of Mama, not a phrase of a little boy ... (*looking at him with tenderness*). My little boy, for shame, it's ugly to put oneself into such states!

OLIVER: And we will know, they will know, and what will I answer?

FRANCES: (*smiling*) Your classmates?—Go on, if you are thinking about what your classmates will say, you do not have a lot of grief. I feared something else ...

OLIVER: (*with vehemence*) Do you believe then that it wouldn't hurt me to think that you, my big sister, you a young girl ...

FRANCES: But you see, my darling, they are words. For in just a few days I will no longer be a maiden anymore.

OLIVER: Ah! Well, your consolations make me feel worse.

FRANCES: (*with resignation*) I have shocked you once again ... By now, however you should be able to get used to it, my boy.

OLIVER: I will never get used to it ... What would our grandparents have said, or even papa, if they had been able to foresee?

FRANCES: And Methuselah, what would he have said? (*Movement of Oliver*) Pardon. But what do you want, it's not my fault, not mine, if time marches forward, I cannot be like an Agnes. I have never been an Agnes. I am sorry because that would have pleased you (*imitating*). The little cat is dead (*Oliver cannot stop himself from laughing*). Go on now, you are laughing; a big fat kiss, and then let's speak no more about it.

OLIVER: I will not forget anything. It is too deep.

Act One: Scene Nine

The same characters; Antoinette, Lucy.

LUCY: (*a "petit four" in her hand, to Antoinette*) I prefer them in pistachio ... What a shame that you have not been able to see her play! And the little Yvonne Létang was charming (*to Frances*). Have you been to see her at her place?

FRANCES: Yes, it amused me ... truly imprudent on my part. But bah! Never mind.

OLIVER: (*in a choked voice*) You have been to see that creature? But when?

FRANCES: Yesterday at four o'clock.

OLIVER: When we believed you were at Aunt Martha's! Oh! A girl who has morals ...

ANTOINETTE: Tell me Oliver, you seem nicely informed ... (*Frances makes a sign for her to keep quiet*).

LUCY: (*to create a diversion ...*) I have an idea, why don't you come for dinner to our house?

FRANCES: And you are forgetting the banquet of the League.

LUCY: It's true, but he can always come to say goodnight to his niece.

ANTOINETTE: Go console yourself by contemplating that innocent face, we are not pure enough for you. (*Oliver leaves with Lucy.*)

Act One: Scene Ten

Antoinette, Frances

FRANCES: Poor child! Basically ...

ANTOINETTE: He's funny.

FRANCES: As for me, he does not amuse me. I know that he will suffer through others and through himself; he is one of those scrupulous and anxious natures that gets upset over nothing.

ANTOINETTE: Tell me: is it because of snobbery that he is with New Youth?

FRANCES: And you, do tell me where does sincerity begin? (*A silence, then brusquely*) Well, we are not worth very much, even the best among us. I have harmed that little one somewhat.

ANTOINETTE: He will console himself. And then how does this concern him?

FRANCES: I envy you taking life with such simplicity.

ANTOINETTE: For a long time I found everything complicated; I was searching to satisfy a thousand exigencies of conscience coming from I don't know where; I was unhappy because it was necessary to put some of it aside. Then one fine day I said to myself: What good is it? And besides where do these scruples come from? Wouldn't we laugh if we knew their origin? You can imagine how I felt relieved.

FRANCES: We are nihilists, Antoinette.

ANTOINETTE: It's quite possible, and then what? It's only a label.

FRANCES: Happy are those who don't reflect too much! ... So really nothing matters?

ANTOINETTE: Yes, one thing: death and beyond.

FRANCES: (*with emotion*) Death! (Enter Mrs. Thouret)

MRS. THOURET: What, Antoinette: you are here and no one told me! How are things going my child? And your mother? You are not too tired from the long journey? What was the crossing like? (*A telegram is brought to Frances who opens it hastily.*) What is it?

FRANCES: It's from Gerard.

MRS. THOURET: He is not coming?

FRANCES: (*reading*) Yes ... Ah! ...

MRS. THOURET: What?

FRANCES: Nothing (*to Antoinette*) you excuse me? (*She rereads feverishly.*)

MRS. THOURET: (*to Antoinette*) I am going to see your mother as soon as possible.

ANTOINETTE: You will find her in every evening after five o'clock, dear madam.

MRS. THOURET: Naturally we are very busy at this time.

ANTOINETTE: Yes ...

MRS. THOURET: The dressmaker is waiting for me, but I wanted to greet you (*she leaves*).

ANTOINETTE: What is it?

FRANCES: I don't understand ... he seems to have written this in a moment of madness. "My darling, I don't know if I will be able to come this evening. What I feared so much has happened!"

ANTOINETTE: What does it mean?

FRANCES: I don't understand. But the following part is terrible: "It's going to be necessary for us to give each other up or at least ... I cannot finish. My heart is breaking. I am writing to you in haste in a post office. It is noisy; I am choking. Why am I writing to you? You will know well soon enough." Antoinette, my Antoinette, what does it mean?

ANTOINETTE: It's incomprehensible; and these lines, incoherent ...

FRANCES: (*with panic*) But it cannot be; my happiness cannot escape me like this.

ANTOINETTE: Calm down.

FRANCES: How do you expect me to be calm before such an enigma, when my life is at stake? You don't understand that it's my life? You don't understand that a delay would drive me crazy, that I love him to distraction? Listen: the other day I was at his place, we had tea together, he said ... I no longer know what, ordinary things perhaps; I was not listening, I was feeling my heart beat wildly. He only has to say the word and I would have given myself to him. I was thinking the whole time: will he say it, this word?

ANTOINETTE: My poor Frances!

FRANCES: No, you see, I am not afraid to be like this; I am probably without modesty, but I don't believe in modesty for those who love: I am proud of loving this way, I feel myself to be more worthy of him (*with terror*). But I discourse at length and you, you are listening, and something has happened that we cannot know; an unknown power of destruction is working to separate us. What could this power be? I only know the fatality of my desire.

ANTOINETTE: (*in spite of everything, embarrassed*) But does he know that you love him like this?

FRANCES: Ah! Do you think that his heart could not read into mine? Those words, I have not said them to him, because it was not worth it. But how could he not guess?

ANTOINETTE: No, well, your silence is explained. Men do not want to be loved like that.

FRANCES: (*sound of bell*) Someone is ringing; my dear Antoinette, goodbye. It is better that you do not meet him. (*Antoinette goes out by the side door.*)

Act One: Scene Eleven

Frances, Gerard

FRANCES: (*trying to restrain herself*) There you are at last! Well! You can boast of having made me distraught; what is this enigma, and why this telegram?

GERARD: (*wearily*) You will know all, my poor Frances.

FRANCES: How pale you are! What is the matter?

GERARD: So you haven't guessed?

FRANCES: No, nothing.

GERARD: (*looking at her fixedly*) Well, I've been to see Perigny.

FRANCES: Perigny? Who is Perigny?

GERARD: You don't know who Perigny is?

FRANCES: No, explain yourself, Gerard, I beg you … It's a doctor it seems, Perigny …

GERARD: Yes, it's a doctor …

FRANCES: I remember now, well?

GERARD: Well! My apprehensions are justified. I am threatened.

FRANCES: Threatened? … By what?

GERARD: The right lung.

FRANCES: (*with a mitigated relief*) That is it! … It's terrible, indeed.

GERARD: You well remember what I have said more than once; I had always feared that there remained traces of my pleurisy, I had bizarre sensations at times ...

FRANCES: I remember ... but this lesion ... this lesion is insignificant.

GERARD: (*with a gesture*) For the time being; but who can know? It'll be necessary that I exile myself, that I lead the life that you know of, that I try to heal to be able to ...

FRANCES: (*with terror*) You wish to delay our marriage, to wait to be healed? No, it's not possible. I will never lend myself to that.

GERARD: (*with a sob*) Do you believe therefore that for me it is not the most bitter of disappointments? Imagine, I reproached myself for getting myself examined.

FRANCES: (*in spite of herself*) Ah! Yes, why ...

GERARD: But now, now that I know ...

FRANCES: (*distraught*) Why didn't you tell me?

GERARD: (*surprised*) What ... You see, my poor darling, we must resign ourselves; I will go bury myself in a sanatorium, and you during that time ... you will marry another.

FRANCES: What are you saying?

GERARD: I cannot hope that you will wait.

FRANCES: (*decisively*) I will not wait. We will marry on the fifteenth (*movement of Gerard*). Listen to me. First of all a delay would be a break. Ah! Pardon me for having uttered this awful word. Mama would no longer wish to hear talk of a marriage between you and I if we did. And if it was only that! ...

GERARD: What do you mean?

MRS. THOURET: (*from the outside*) You are here, Gerard! Come say hello to me. (*He goes to the door and opens it.*)

FRANCES: (*with terror, to herself*) "Only one thing matters, it's death." He could disappear without me ever having been his ...

GERARD: (*returning*) What were you saying?

FRANCES: Nothing, I no longer remember ... Listen to me ... (*hesitating*). There is a decisive reason (*triumphantly*), decisive: it's that far from me, alone among sick people, you would not be cured. Do you believe that I don't know you? Do you believe that I don't remember what you told me in the old days about your despair when you left your mother?

GERARD: (*moved*) It's true.

FRANCES: (*ardently*) From the dejection which seized you ... do you believe that I don't know how much you would suffer ... And the horrible thoughts that would cross your mind ... You would say to yourself: I will never see her, never again.

GERARD: It's true; one must only think of death in those places.

FRANCES: Of death ... Do you think that the thought of death is not fatal for a soul such as yours, a sensitive soul? I see you during the interminable afternoons on the chaise lounge; and at night ...

GERARD: (*with despair*) But Frances, it is necessary, however you cannot marry a sick person. Your mother ...

FRANCES: Mama will know nothing.

GERARD: Have you the right to hide it from her? ...

FRANCES: Have I the right to inflict upon her the torments, the anguish that you cannot even suspect?

GERARD: Do you think that I don't suspect them?

FRANCES: No, my darling, you must be reasonable and not get carried away; certainly it's very serious; but how could you have thought? ... I truly believe that you didn't remember that I loved you.

GERARD: (*with intoxication*) You love me ...

FRANCES: (*in spite of herself, maternally*) You know very well that we love you, big baby. We will leave together as soon as possible, we will rent a chalet in Switzerland ... Do you believe that we won't be happy? And don't you think that you will get better in this way?

GERARD: (*not being able to contain his joy*) Frances!

FRANCES: Do you think that happiness doesn't do any good ... more good than a serum?

GERARD: Who knows? Perigny is perhaps mistaken ...

FRANCES: No, Perigny has not made a mistake. But you should not take this revelation tragically, panic, and do something wrong.

GERARD: But I believe truly that I do not have the right ...

FRANCES: (*violently*) You do not have the right to say no (*with effort*). Have you thought of what my life would be during that time? The terror at each opened letter? And all the horror of a life suspended in anguish, of a life arrested!

GERARD: It's true ... and you don't know how much I will need you so that I do not become discouraged. I have so much faith in your courage, in the power of your spiritual radiance ... I know you are so virile, so lofty ...

FRANCES: (*in a low voice*) Really?

GERARD: I have faith in you, Frances.

FRANCES: (*to herself*) I don't know what faith is, not even faith in oneself. Or rather it is only ever fraudulence.

GERARD: (*involuntarily*) Oh! Do not speak like that about faith.

FRANCES: Why such revolt?

GERARD: It seems to me that love can work miracles.

FRANCES: (*deeply*) My poor friend, love is a force of nature, nothing more.

GERARD: Of nature? Who knows? My darling, I would like to see in you more fervor.

FRANCES: (*weary*) Some fervor now? Come now, we are here discussing love as if we were not in love. Come close to me (*he approaches and seizes the hand of Frances; the evening begins to descend*). Do you want me to turn on the light?

GERARD: No, no, not yet.

FRANCES: (*speaking so as to remind Gerard to hide his illness from others for the time being*) Hello, Gerard. You just now arrived! Do not forget.

GERARD: (*lending himself to it*) If you wish.

FRANCES: It's with another, with a stranger that I have just spoken; you do not know him; I am not introducing him to you. We have said things without interest.

GERARD: (*sadly*) It's a sick man.

FRANCES: No, not this word; do not forget that I love him. If you wish, just now I will sing for you La Chevelure; I know it now.

GERARD: No, not tonight.

FRANCES: Why not tonight?

GERARD: (*without answering*) Frances, it's true that you love me? ... I feel so unworthy of you, with all my dirty past (*gesture of Frances.*) You think you know but you do not know. One day I will tell you, and we will cry together.

FRANCES: Why will we cry? My friend, why do you torment yourself like this?

GERARD: Frances, I feel such a need for purity at the moment beside you.

FRANCES: (*with veiled irony that he does not notice*) I inspire you with thoughts of purity?

GERARD: You do not know what you are and what you can be for me: the counselor, the messenger.

FRANCES: (*with fright*) Really!

GERARD: To be pure, I would like to be pure.

FRANCES: No one is absolutely pure.

GERARD: (*with anguish*) You think so? It's true ... I have never been pure.

FRANCES: Look; in the distance the sky is fading; Paris is disappearing in a delighful way.

GERARD: That recalls to me another evening ... I will tell you about it sometime. My God! What disgust! (*Frances looks at him with a surprise mixed with pity*.) Frances, play me something, but no Debussy this evening.

FRANCES: Something pure.

GERARD: Yes, something pure.

FRANCES: Why don't you play yourself, my darling? I love it when you play; leave the door ajar; I'll hear fine from here (*he goes into a side room, Frances sits down and leans her face on her hand, she looks thoughtful and sad*).

(*Gerard attacks the first measures of the piece of the air from Pater Marianus in the third part of Schumann's* Faust.)

MRS. THOURET: (*half-opening the door*) Who is playing?

FRANCES: It's Gerard.

MRS. THOURET: What was the meaning of the little blue letter?

FRANCES: Nothing. I no longer remember.

(*Mrs. Thouret goes out; we no longer hear music*.)

FRANCES: Why has he stopped playing? (*She goes to the door and looks in*.) (*With fright*) It looks like he is praying!

CURTAIN

ACT TWO

The scene is at the home of the Launoys; small bright living-room of the newlyweds. In the background French doors which open onto the balcony. Doors to the right and to the left.

Act Two: Scene One

Mrs. Thouret, Lucy, a maid

MRS. THOURET: A spitting of blood? You are sure, Martha?

THE MAID: Yes, madam, quite sure because I saw that Mr. ...

MRS. THOURET: It's frightening. You heard, Lucy?

LUCY: Yes, Mama. It's frightful.

MRS. THOURET: And you've been for the doctor?

THE MAID: No, madam, John went for him.

MRS. THOURET: But what did the doctor say? You don't know naturally.

LUCY: It's maddening.

MRS. THOURET: Frances will tell us everything ...

THE MAID: Madam will come immediately. (*She goes out.*)

MRS. THOURET: What do you say about it?

LUCY: I am upset.

MRS. THOURET: Who could expect that? Clearly I knew he was delicate; but from that to suspect ...

Gabriel Marcel

LUCY: You believe therefore that he is ...

MRS. THOURET: My poor child. A spitting of blood, it is clear. I recall now that he coughed sometimes ... But could I think of having him examined by a physician? And then would I have dared to ask it of him?

LUCY: Who knows if he ignored it?

MRS. THOURET: How can you suppose him capable of such a monstrosity?

LUCY: Oh! You know, men! (*A silence; Mrs. Thouret sighs deeply.*)

MRS. THOURET: My God! What wretchedness!

Act Two: Scene Two

The same characters; Frances

MRS. THOURET: My poor child! What Martha just told me! I beg you, spare me your lamentations!

LUCY: But when did it happen?

FRANCES: Last night; he wanted with all his strength to read me his latest verses, a work on the stars; he got excited, and in the middle of his reading ...

MRS. THOURET: What a horrible thing!

LUCY: But it seems that this does not always prove that he is stricken. The little Lecharmont girl ...

MRS. THOURET: The case is quite different.

LUCY: I assure you mama ...

FRANCES: He is stricken.

MRS. THOURET: (*as if it was a revelation*) He is stricken? My God! What wretchedness!

FRANCES: Let's see Mama, you see that I am calm. When you take a disease at the beginning...

MRS. THOURET: He is stricken!

FRANCES: There is no need for panic. It's very serious, but on condition of doing all that is necessary ...

MRS. THOURET: It's true when one takes a disease at its beginning ...

LUCY: Yes, when one takes it in time ...

MRS. THOURET: All the same, what wretchedness! ... And so what are you going to do, my poor children? It's going to be necessary for you to separate!

LUCY: It's true.

FRANCES: (*distinctly*) It is out of the question!

MRS. THOURET: You are not going to send him to a sanatorium?

FRANCES: Everything is already decided. He does not want a sanatorium, and I do not want it either.

MRS. THOURET: Then again ...

FRANCES: (*as if to herself*) No, it will not be said that my madness has been in vain ...

MRS. THOURET: (*quite softly*) She regrets, the poor child ...

FRANCES: We will rent a chalet in the neighborhood of a sanatorium, in order to have medical care, air, everything after all.

MRS. THOURET: (*terrified*) You are not thinking. And contagion?

FRANCES: When one takes the necessary precautions, there is no contagion possible.

LUCY: I have always heard said however …

FRANCES: And furthermore that would not stop me. The tie that binds us is stronger than life.

MRS. THOURET: My darling, allow me to tell you that they are words. You owe yourself to all of us—to him who needs to find you in good health later on—to me—to another perhaps.

FRANCES: (*laughing with excitement*) No, do not worry, my good mama; it is not a question of that at the moment.—Now, listen, it is better that I remain alone. First of all, I am afraid that the noise might awaken him … He is sleeping beside … (*painfully*) He is sleeping … he is very tired.

MRS. THOURET: My God! What wretchedness. (*She goes out with Lucy.*)

Act Two: Scene Three

Frances is alone, then Antoinette

FRANCES: (*to herself*) Contagion! It's a question of contagion! (*She sits lost in painful reflections.*)

ANTOINETTE: (*entering*) (*at half-voice*) I'm staying only a minute … I know … Your mother told me everything … My dear one. (*She kisses her.*)

FRANCES: It does me good to see you … I cannot cry when I am alone. (*She cries.*)

ANTOINETTE: But how did it happen? This frightful surprise …

FRANCES: It has not been a surprise.—I was expecting it, I should have expected what has happened.

ANTOINETTE: What do you mean?

FRANCES: Do you remember the little blue letter that I received the day that you came back from Egypt?

ANTOINETTE: Yes, you did not want to tell me what it was.

FRANCES: I was afraid that you might not know how to keep the secret. Well! Since that day I knew that Gerard was consumptive.

ANTOINETTE: So that was it! It was why you didn't tell me ...

FRANCES: You judge me mad to have married him anyway ...

ANTOINETTE: No, it was in the order of things ...

FRANCES: I saw our union pushed back, rendered impossible. Death occurring without my having become his, without this passionate desire that I had for him being realized.

ANTOINETTE: Yes, I understand.

FRANCES: No, you cannot know my distress; I remembered your sentence: Only one thing matters, it's death ... And the fear of seeing my happiness fly away forever, I wanted to embrace him (*wild*), embrace him immediately. But I have expiated this madness. There are things it seems that I am not able to tell you ... You are still a young girl.

ANTOINETTE: (*bitterly*) You think so?

FRANCES: But you can guess, perhaps ... the terror that seized me at certain moments; the fear of seeing emerge after nights of love the sickness that I knew was pursuing in him its dark path. And so the will to moderate ...

ANTOINETTE: Yes.

FRANCES: You have grasped it. And not once (*with a kind of despair*) not once have we been truly … lovers … Then, one evening in Italy, I came back and I found his face convulsed, changed, oh! So changed … oh! That frightful face, that face of one hundred years! (*She cries.*) At first he wanted to keep out of sight, but his faint voice, his dead voice told me everything; and he began to cry like a child.

GERARD: (*from the wings*) Frances, Frances!

FRANCES: (*running to the door*) What is it?

GERARD: (*from the wings*) I'm feeling better; I'll get up shortly.

FRANCES: Good, my darling; I am waiting for you with Antoinette. (*She comes back.*)

ANTOINETTE: It's awful, all of it!

FRANCES: Ah, if it was only that! But there's the rest; all that I only dimly glimpse …

ANTOINETTE: Do you think that I cannot guess, my poor Frances, the tragic misunderstanding which separates both of you? Come now, the experience of love is not necessary to know love. From that distant day when I returned from Egypt I foresaw what would happen. You both do not love in the same way. The man whose ardors have calmed is not able to understand the transports of the young lover; he is seeking the woman in her and she wants to find a lover in him.

FRANCES: (*with anguish*) No, no, it's not only that; it's not only the banal drama that you say. Other forces are at work, which are more powerful than my will, impose on me a detestable role.

ANTOINETTE: What do you mean?

Act Two: Scene Four

The same characters; Gerard

(*Gerard opens the door on the right; he is pale and visibly very weak; Frances casts a glance at her friend almost ashamedly and full of anguish; neither he nor Antoinette notice it*)

ANTOINETTE: (*getting up*) Hello, Sir.

GERARD: No, stay, please, Miss. I know what joy Frances feels when seeing you; you are her only intimate friend. And her life beside the invalid that I am is so sad, that she doubly needs around her the presence of those dear to her. Besides, if you don't mind, Frances, I'd like to say a word to your friend.

FRANCES: (*with surprise*) Am I in the way?

GERARD: I'd like to remain alone for five minutes with the young lady.

ANTOINETTE: So, Frances, your husband is compromising me!

(*Frances has a sad smile; she goes out onto the balcony.*)

GERARD: (*lowering his voice, to Antoinette*) Miss, I know what you mean to Frances, she has an absolute confidence in you; there are things that you alone can say to her; there are things that (*sadly*) she has only said to you (*gesture of Antoinette*). You are also the only one who can advise her ... (*he stops*).

ANTOINETTE: What do you mean?

GERARD: When I am here no longer.

ANTOINETTE: But what makes you able to believe that?

GERARD: They can speak of hopes, of a sure cure; I feel, I know that I am lost. We are going to leave for Montana (*with tenderness*) because she wants to, because she would not forgive herself for doing nothing. What does it matter to me after all to die here or there? Provided that she be beside me. For I still have the frightful egotism of those who do not want to be alone at the moment of expiring. There she will have at least the illusion of caring for me; quickly she'll notice that the air does me good, that I am regaining some strength, what do I know? But I cannot get well (*with a kind of concentrated fervor*) and I do not want to get well.

ANTOINETTE: I do not understand.

FRANCES: (*from the balcony*) You haven't finished talking yet?

GERARD: (*in a low voice*) I barely understand myself; and I don't feel the need to understand myself. The indistinct and deep voice that I hear within me is of those who are not able to deceive. What I know is that the act by which Frances renounced happiness, the act of supreme charity by which she accepted living with an invalid ...

ANTOINETTE: (*deeply troubled*) Yes ...

GERARD: That act basically condemned me to death. Even cured, I would remain a fragile individual over whom one must keep watch; I owe myself, I owe her the deliverance from a useless being who takes her life and her strength. You do not seem to understand ...

ANTOINETTE: No, I fear I do not understand.

GERARD: So she told you? ... But then ... Would you think it fair that she be paid for her sacrifice by a life of nursing?

FRANCES: (*who has come back*) The joy of sacrifice excludes any reward.

GERARD: (*reproachfully*) You listened to us!

FRANCES: (*to Antoinette*) You don't know what he means to tell you; and I have guessed it; he wishes that later on (*she breaks into sobs*) you persuade me not to be faithful to his memory ... Ah! Don't say another word; these forecasts are atrocious, and the thought of death is not that of those who sustain life (*to Gerard*). Come my beloved, I'll settle you on the balcony (*she leads Gerard onto the balcony and settles him in, then she returns after closing the door*).

ANTOINETTE: I do not understand. What is this story about sacrifice?

FRANCES: (*with a bitter smile*) Naturally you do not understand, because you know me and you know the situation. The act of supreme charity, the sacrifice of which he speaks with emotion, is in reality the most egotistical act of my life. He does not know the unbridled desire, irresistible, that led me to him.

ANTOINETTE: I remember those dissimulations which surprised me ...

FRANCES: He does not know that I would rather die than not become his, even if only for one hour.

ANTOINETTE: (*with surprise*) What, you never revealed your passion, even when you were in his arms?

FRANCES: Do you remember the anguish that I felt in those moments ... and then I resisted my desire, I didn't dare to ask for his caresses again, for fear of seeming impure to him. What he loves in me is a chaste and fearful stranger that I do not know; I trembled on the day that for the first time I understood what strange image he had of me and loved instead of me. And then, moved by I don't know what irresistible force, I began to apply myself with all my might to resemble this false image. Do you understand now my pain? Do you understand what it is for me to be obliged to lie to myself, and to lie to the one that I love more than myself, when sincerity is the only duty that I have ever understood, the only one that I have ever practiced?

ANTOINETTE: What does it matter in general? Aren't souls impenetrable to each other? What is the point of wanting to be known as one is? And do you know yourself so well to know what you are?

FRANCES: Unfortunately!

ANTOINETTE: Believe me, life is simple for he who does not refine in detail his feelings like this.

FRANCES: There are hours when it seems to me that love cannot resist the lie.

ANTOINETTE: (*looking at her*) Are you sure that it always resists realities? (*A silence; the window-door opens.*)

GERARD: It's beginning to get cold.

ANTOINETTE: (*getting up*) This time, I must be going. I'll try to come back soon. (*Frances accompanies her to the door; Gerard sits down.*)

Act Two: Scene Five

Frances, Gerard

GERARD: I like the honest face of your friend; but why didn't she seem to understand what I said?

FRANCES: I don't know.

GERARD: She doesn't measure the expanse of your sacrifice.

FRANCES: Ah! Do not always speak of that (*harshly*). I was not sacrificing myself because I loved you.

GERARD: There are so many ways to love!

FRANCES: (*painfully*) I am beginning to believe it.

GERARD: What do you mean my darling? I fear I understand you.

FRANCES: (*sharply*) No, no.

GERARD: Why wish to erase the veiled reproach which was piercing through your words? Go on, I had only guessed your repugnance for ...

FRANCES: For?

GERARD: For physical love. When you used to slip out of my embrace you were revealing the innate purity of your being ... And it is since then that I understood all that you were worth ... Frances, I love your almost fanatical chastity.

FRANCES: (*to herself*) It's too pitiful ...

GERARD: I can tell you everything now; before I seemed to find in you I don't know what strange passion which offended me. How much I was mistaken!

FRANCES: (*weakly*) Yes.

GERARD: Come now, you do not know what an assistant you have been for me in this work of purification which is being carried out in me.

FRANCES: Let's talk of something else, shall we?

GERARD: Only one word. This confession that you required of all my detestable past has forced me to face all the evil that I have done, all the evil that I did to myself.

FRANCES: (*in spite of herself*) So what do you know, unfortunate one, of the curiosity that drove me to know all about your life? (*Forcing herself to speak jokingly*) Who knows if I am not depraved?

GERARD: (*who hasn't listened to her*) Just now I was watching those children who were playing under the chestnut trees, and I said to myself: Those children, are they already impure? My God, is it possible that the curse of the centuries be upon them, and that already the spirit of lust is at work in the depths of their uncertain hearts?

FRANCES: You are harming yourself my darling; you should not talk so much.

GERARD: I never told you how desire revealed itself to me (*troubling himself*), and perhaps I should not tell that to you. Those children who were playing in the garden reminded me of someone long ago who once awakened a dormant passion within me. I was sixteen years old. It was the son of a friend of my mother, he had big blond curls, his blue eyes were smiling, he spoke little and his mother complained sometimes that he was not intelligent. The message of the deep eyes, it seems to me that I understand it now. But then I felt myself troubled to the depths of my soul by the mysterious purity of that look … and however, alas! That purity only aroused in me impure thoughts … I am wrong to tell you this, my poor Frances … I never spoke to him and I always feared that someone might discover the dubious affection that I felt for him. I didn't know myself exactly what I wanted; I didn't understand myself, and yet I felt that love was awakened in me. He died when eleven years old, I cried … Could it be that at the bottom of the most troubling desires there has always been the invincible and hidden allure of purity?

FRANCES: (*shaking her head*) No, no, desire destroys itself and is reborn from its own destruction to destroy itself again, it is eternal fever, eternal anguish. The poor and pitiful tragedy, only death concludes.

GERARD: (*with sweetness*) Perhaps death is only a beginning (*a silence …* *he continues*). So then, the more the carnal and vain life that I have lived becomes foreign to me, the more I convince myself that the world to which I aspire and for which I feel myself created is not this one.

FRANCES: (*with bitterness*) This existence then, would only be a test imposed on our inexpert wills imposed by—I don't know what kind of demanding and whimsical master? Does such an approach therefore place before your eyes the value of life, or rather make it a contest instituted by some idle pedant? (*With continued and deep pain.*) No, no, there are those who take life tragically. And they are the only ones who are worth anything, those who have known the terrible thrill of risk, they well know there is no other existence than ours. There is only one part to play, too bad for whoever wastes it.

GERARD: (*mysteriously*) May the One that you ignore reveal to you someday the madness of your presumption and your blasphemy, Frances.

FRANCES: My poor friend, I fear I have passed the age of conversion.

GERARD: (*with fright*) What could have made you this premature old soul?

FRANCES: (*changing the conversation*) I didn't tell you that I wrote this morning to the two doctors over there. I first thought of going to the site by myself, but I couldn't resign myself to leaving you alone.

GERARD: (*profoundly*) What does it matter! And why come recalling those little details? It's necessary that before the final goodbye we've had at least once the courage to look at ourselves.

FRANCES: (*with fright*) No, what good is it?

GERARD: (*with tenderness*) My poor Frances, do you believe that I hold it against you to remain foreign to this faith which slowly has taken root in me? It is this faith, the unforeseen gift from an unknown spiritual power that has heard the call of my misery and my impurity; it is grace.

FRANCES: (*remembering*) Grace ...

GERARD: It is living testimony from the One from whom it emanates; it carries his seal. But (*with infinite tenderness*) the unbeliever who sacrificed herself without the hope of recompense, do you believe then that she cannot hope for infinite mercy?

FRANCES: (*disgusted*) Mercy ... There are poor people who do not accept alms.

GERARD: Go on, the sublime ingenuousness of your sacrifice remains whole, and that alone matters. In spite of yourself you have let yourself be permeated by the spirit of charity which blows across the world and which renders it worthy of divine clemency.

FRANCES: Forgiveness is made for mediocre and floating souls; for others, for those who have chosen freely and forever, forgiveness is an outrage.

GERARD: My God, make her humble herself before your omnipotence.

FRANCES: God Himself cannot force love.

Act Two: Scene Six

The same characters; Oliver

OLIVER: (*going to Gerard*) How do you feel now, Gerard?

GERARD: (*smiling*) Better, my friend, thank you.

OLIVER: Mama has not recovered from her emotional upset; she sent me the news.

GERARD: Let's not speak of these miseries. What must be, will be; what good is it to torment oneself and to complain? The disease will continue its work, whatever we do.

OLIVER: What is this pessimism? And you, Frances, you let Gerard get discouraged like this? (*Gesture of Frances*) You must want to get better, and you will get better.

GERARD: The need to live, I no longer feel it (*Frances throws a desperate look at Oliver*).

OLIVER: I do not understand you. Life! All the marvelous possibilities of action and of enthusiasm that this word suggests, you abdicate them lightheartedly?

GERARD: The truth cannot be in action that disperses and degrades. It is in the fervent concentration of the soul lost to love and veneration that I perceive the good to which I aspire.

FRANCES: (*with a bitter sadness*) Gerard has become a mystic.

GERARD: One does not become mystic; and I am discovering seeds of religion in all the follies of my past. But now I would no longer be able to accept the perpetual distractions of this life. (*He closes his eyes.*)

FRANCES: (*at half-voice*) Isn't he unrecognizable?

OLIVER: (*with ardor*) But religions like yours are not those which make life better.

GERARD: Life cannot be made better only through human forces.

OLIVER: So be it, but active and conquering faiths, aren't they worth more than that of the mystic lost in his ecstasy?

GERARD: The choice was not left to me.

OLIVER: But again I've never heard you talk like this ... yet I suspected behind your words the mysterious sprouting seed of belief. I like you better, Gerard, as a believer; (*with regret*) if I had your faith, what wouldn't I do! But alas! The grace that seems to have touched you, I am still waiting for it.

FRANCES: Which doesn't stop you from taking part in all the church services. Sincerity is not one of the virtues of your group.

OLIVER: (*looking at her*) Who then can say he is entirely sincere? And isn't it possible to simply fight for that which one loves and which one reveres? (*Becoming animated*) Am I responsible for a skepticism that all the fatal education which I have received has worked to implant in me? And will I have to bear the weight of it all my life? Besides, the more the faith is alive, the less the merit is great. Honor to those ignited by the beauty of the idea!

GERARD: Oliver, I sense coming through your words, anxiety about God.

OLIVER: (*with emotion*) Who could explain the happy spiritual effects of illness! Perhaps God only reveals Himself to the weak and infirm.

FRANCES: Reverie of a man in good health!

OLIVER: Why wouldn't illness develop in us spiritual senses foreign to the normal man?

FRANCES: We see that you hardly know about what a brain is, and how much the slightest cause suffices to trouble its functioning.

OLIVER: You speak about thought like a watchmaker about a clock.

GERARD: (*lost in his meditations*) If disease were always a good and always carried with it its spiritual justification ... !

OLIVER: Someone said that the real cause of an evil could never be of the physical order.

FRANCES: My poor friends, you are talking nonsense.

OLIVER: You could call your friend Du Ryer to the rescue, he would speak to us a little about the digestive tubes.

GERARD: If it were true however! (*with ecstasy*) If all the physical miseries that we suffer with moaning, had their reason for being in a higher and invisible order, and were only ever the instruments of providential wisdom ...

FRANCES: Spare me this language from the catechism. I see that you are tired. You should go back to bed.

OLIVER: (*smiling*) For once listen to the language of this godless one.

FRANCES: Call me as soon as you need me. (*He leaves.*)

Act Two: Scene Seven

Frances, Oliver

FRANCES: (*anxiously*) How do you find him? Quite changed, right?

OLIVER: What surprises me most is this sudden outpouring of all that one was only sensing within him.

FRANCES: (*bitterly*) I have been able to follow, alas, the gradual development of his mysticism.

OLIVER: Why do you lament that a faith, of which we all have so much need, should awaken in him?

FRANCES: How could I regret not sharing his illusions? I have not yet fallen so low. But it is not about that. In this disgust for life wherein he thinks to see the longing for another world, I read only too clearly the approaching annihilation; and his aspirations for immortality are only to my impartial reasoning but the illusory flames of a heart that is going to be extinguished.

OLIVER: So who are you to judge and to deny? Where do you get this science of life and death? Is it in laboratories that one acquires it? Why (*with ardor*), why wouldn't the physical order be the symbolic and imperfect expression of another order? Why would illusion always be on the side of those who believe and who hope? By what right do you forbid God to imprint, on the sufferings of our bodies, a spiritual meaning which ennobles and transfigures them? It's a poor wisdom that professes to impose limits on Divine power.

FRANCES: This aesthetic attraction that faith exerts on unbelieving and soft souls like yours. When religion is not for you a simple means of government, it degenerates until it is no more than a spiritual ornament; but never, in no case do you treat it as a reality.

OLIVER: (*flaring up*) Even if a faith like that of Gerard would be an illusion, it would be more respectable than your truth.

FRANCES: Ah! You acknowledge it then. This respect for the truth which rests with us, the sensual and helpless ones, you no longer possess it. Disgusted with reality, unable to face it, you are weaving I don't know what illusory doctrine which throws over your cowardice a cover of idealism. We are better than you because we refuse to see the world other than it is, nor our souls as better than they are. Sincerity ...

OLIVER: (*bitingly*) It's the second time today that you have used this word. Is it for you to talk about sincerity, you who in order to please your husband have concealed the impure desires of which your heart is full?

FRANCES: Oliver!

OLIVER: Oh, haven't you always been honest with me? You, who playing the chaste spouse, the cerebral and cold woman, have hidden from him the unhealthy obsessions and the depraved imaginings in which you have indulged?

FRANCES: (*in tears*) Oliver, what have I done to you for you to talk to me like that? Is this how you respond to my kindness? Must I, on the threshold of a life of trials of which I do not perceive the term, hear these atrocious words and that it is you who address them to me?

OLIVER: (*with hardness*) Aren't they truths?

FRANCES: What do you know of what I have suffered? What do you know of the nights of insomnia and anguish that I have spent?

OLIVER: I have no pity for you, you only reap what you have sown.

FRANCES: Spare me this old refrain.

OLIVER: The books that you have read, the teachers you have had, the friends with which you have surrounded yourself, this Antoinette above all, your favorite, all have contributed to make of you the sensual, reasoning, and presumptuous creature in her negations that you are today. Strangely, the perverse desires which consume you have found (*ironically*) in your mind the most obedient of servants. I remember the hateful curiosities that you would go to the dictionaries of physiology and medicine to gratify; we marveled to see you so anxious to know; in reality you were looking for a justification for the demands … of your nature. And I remember you coming back from the theater trembling, shaken by sobs, obsessed by the depraved tragedies to which they had the poor judgment to take you, basically happy to see everywhere a victorious sensuality, the same that you found all powerful in the depths of your being. (*Seeing Frances livid.*) Ah! Pardon for speaking like this. But do you think that I haven't suffered from all of it?

FRANCES: (*vehemently*) How about me? Do you think it's from gaiety of heart that I have become all that you say?

OLIVER: I don't want to know about the crises that you have experienced; I guess only too well; didn't you once have more modesty towards me about certain desires and anxieties! I remember the day when for the first time you read me your lines of poetry; it was in the garden at Sèvres, an afternoon in July. It began like this: "Beloved, I will be your immodest slave"; And this line: "Your caresses will never be too passionate." And you were reading that so calmly! …

FRANCES: I remember your surprised look. My poor dear! All of it seemed so natural to me.

OLIVER: (*sadly*) I know … Those lines, does Gerard know them?

FRANCES: (*again hostile*) What does it matter to you?

OLIVER: There are accommodations with sincerity.

FRANCES: Gerard is an invalid; I am obliged to care for him. Do you think I wouldn't prefer to tell him everything?

OLIVER: When he recovers ...

FRANCES: Alas! Will he recover?

OLIVER: He'll hear some beauties!

FRANCES: What is all this irony? Would you like me to prolong a deceit that just now you were reproaching me for? What is the meaning of these contradictions? ... And besides, I don't know why I care about your opinion, after your tirade just now when you know nothing of what happened?

OLIVER: Ah! There are things that I don't know? ... (*A silence*) I have nothing to answer you. Your situation is that of those who have no way out; you will never have the courage to inflict on him the deep disappointment that he would feel to see you as you are, and on the other hand it is inevitable that one day your nature will regain the upper hand and that he will perceive his mistake.

FRANCES: His mistake! Ah! No, never that! His mistake ...

OLIVER: It would seem that this word takes on a deeper meaning for you (*she does not respond*). Don't worry, reality is beyond the dilemmas in which we claim to imprison it. Who knows if in three months you will still exist for him?

FRANCES: (*with fright*) What do you mean?

OLIVER: How could one who lives in God still have a thought for a miserable and rebellious creature like you?

FRANCES: What, it's the future that would be reserved for me after my sacrifice ... (*she does not finish*).

OLIVER: What were you saying?

FRANCES: Nothing, a habit ...

OLIVER: Whether you like it or not, the powers with which you are going to have to struggle and whose unknowing plaything you may be, are not the ones that your life has taught you to know.

FRANCES: (*furiously*) I deny them.

OLIVER: May you not become the victim that they have reserved for themselves!

CURTAIN

ACT THREE

The chalet where the Launoys live in Montana. Living room with lacquered furniture; no angles. Everything is in windows. We can see snow shining under the streetlights, and in the background, the Palace illuminated. We indistinctly hear ballroom music.

Act Three: Scene One

Frances, Mrs. Thouret, Gerard, Father Andre

(To the right, Gerard is lying down. Father Andre is seated near to him. To the left Frances and her mother are leaning on the table and chatting softly.)

GERARD: *(to Father Andre)* So your wife took the veil when she was sure that God had called you?

FATHER ANDRE: She felt that it was necessary. But she was one of those weak souls who repent of their best actions because they don't recognize themselves in them. One day she left the convent.

GERARD: What became of her? Did she forgive you her fate?

FATHER ANDRE: *(correcting him)* I have no doubt that God has forgiven her. Every day I pray for her.

FRANCES: *(to her mother)* You heard?

MRS. THOURET: Be careful. Should we say Father or Pastor sir to a missionary?

FRANCES: I know nothing about that.

GERARD: I thank you profoundly for your story. You cannot know how much it has impassioned me. What strikes me most is the suddenness of your conversion.

FATHER ANDRE: Nothing is sudden, only in appearance. In reality, it was resolved from all eternity that I would return one day from my wanderings; no doubt for a sharper view than our ...

MRS. THOURET: *(to Frances)* When did you make his acquaintance?

FRANCES: About a month ago. Gerard was struck by the beauty of his gaze, by the power of its radiance—I quote his words—it emanated from him; what do I know? They spoke to each other; and now they are inseparable. This is the last step.

MRS. THOURET: What do you mean?

FRANCES: Grace will soon have completed its work of destruction. All that I have loved, all that I have desired, all will be torn from me.

MRS. THOURET: Grace?

FRANCES: Didn't you know that your son-in-law was touched by grace?

GERARD: So you have decided to leave again in a week?

FATHER ANDRE: I am now recovered, I feel the strength again to take a trip, it will be the last.

GERARD: I will never see you again (*a sign of negation by Father Andre confirming he will not*).

FATHER ANDRE: I am certain to not return.

FRANCES: He is going to leave.

MRS. THOURET: If you are telling the truth, I am delighted. It is useless to entertain his fanaticism.

FRANCES: (*with fatalism*) The decisive influence of this meeting will extend indefinitely over our life.

GERARD: You cannot know what essential importance it is for me—all that you have told me; this meeting was what it took to convince me fully.

FATHER ANDRE: This is but an external sign.

GERARD: You have brought me the brilliant confirmation of my premonitions. No doubt (*with a mystical fervor*) there is not one of our acts that doesn't have its destination; there is not one of our gestures which doesn't have on other destinies an impact that we might not suspect, but that God has foreseen, that He has wished. But sometimes God paternally consents to let us perceive something of his plans ... I understand why he wanted us to meet.

MRS. THOURET: (*looking at Gerard*) He doesn't look ill tonight.

FRANCES: (*flatly*) He's excited; he'll have a temperature tomorrow.

GERARD: But is it possible that my presumption is not unforgiveable, is it possible that God lavishes his favors on an unworthy one such as I?

FATHER ANDRE: Your past errors contribute to the glory of God by highlighting the abundance of grace that has been given to you.

GERARD: (*with sadness*) No, it's not possible: God could not have wished for evil.

FATHER ANDRE: Evil is not for the one who sees all; the dissonance is lost in the universal harmony to which it contributes.

GERARD: No, I do not want to reason; I believe, my God, I believe in you.

FRANCES: We were forced to give up on overfeeding. He was having atrocious digestive problems.

MRS. THOURET: But you assure me that he has gained weight?

FATHER ANDRE: Who knows? Perhaps the inert belief that still satisfies you will no longer satisfy you in a few months.

GERARD: No, no ... Besides in a few months I will no longer be alive.

FATHER ANDRE: (looking at him with authority) You have a few good years for sure; maybe more. What will you do when you leave Montana? You'll take up again that vain existence with which you say you've broken, and you'll lead, with a heart tormented by remorse, a life that only ignorance could render excusable.

GERARD: I do not want to wonder, I do not want to reflect ... I am still dazzled by the clarity of what has happened (pleading). Why try to make me forget that I'm happy?

FATHER ANDRE: You must not give in to this foolhardy satisfaction; the eye of God is upon you.

GERARD: No, do not speak like that. All will be as it has been ordained from all eternity; my God, let me surrender myself into your loving arms. For all eternity. That phrase cradles one like music.

FATHER ANDRE: Beware of the abyss that awaits the predestined.

MRS. THOURET: He could really have refrained from inviting this gentleman the evening of my arrival.

FRANCES: Oh! If you think he thought of it! When one travels through heaven, one doesn't worry about details like that. He listens to Father Andre like someone taking morphine.

MRS. THOURET: Frances!

FRANCES: A narcotic of the soul, in the end it amounts to the same thing.

MRS. THOURET: This doesn't give me the impression that he has converted you.

FRANCES: Who do you take me for? Come on, this is no laughing matter (*pointing to Gerard*); the collapse of my life is taking place right now.

MRS. THOURET: Why this pessimism? He's better now.

FRANCES: It's not about that. A wall is going up between us. Death itself cannot separate as completely. We cry for the dead, and I no longer exist for him ... (*she stops*).

GERARD: No, even if one day she was born to God, I could not do it. In spite of your affirmations, it seems to me that I would never want to separate myself from the one who sacrificed herself for me.

FRANCES: Did you hear this awful phrase? After what I've endured, moreover, it seems to me that nothing matters any more (*she is silent*).

MRS. THOURET: My poor darling, I understand your anguish.

FRANCES: No, you don't know, you cannot even guess (*in a sudden movement of desperate confidence*). Ah! I regret not telling you everything before. Perhaps you would have been able to advise me. Mama (*she is going to cry*) ... (*in a choked voice*) You realize, right? How much I loved him ... How ... No, you cannot understand.

MRS. THOURET: (*painfully*) Yes, I understand.

FRANCES: I loved him, loved ... well! I've seen my love crumble and fall into pieces. You don't know what an invalid is.

MRS. THOURET: Frances, I've cared for your father for ten years.

FRANCES: (*involuntarily*) You didn't love him like a lover ... Think about it. A lover. A lover of whom one gradually grows disgusted.

MRS. THOURET: (*in spite of herself*) A man is not only an instrument of pleasure.

FRANCES: (*astonished by the word*) You are talking like us, mama! If at least I could have been, I don't know, the nurse, the sister of charity who has pity on the suffering and who consoles them with a gentle look! But I wasn't able to become that soul. If you knew the awful clairvoyance with which I followed the progress of the disease that has withered his flesh. Excuse me, mama.

MRS. THOURET: They didn't teach you kindness.

FRANCES: Alas, maybe one day I'll feel more than pity for him but, it will be done, my love ... But no, that will not be; he's rich in faith and hope and has no need of my tears. And I, I only have my love, which is dying like a child shivering in my arms, powerless to warm it up.

GERARD: (*to Father Andre*) No, I feel within myself neither the courage nor even the desire to imitate you. My certainty is not of those who take communion, and I would desecrate my faith by trying to spread it.

FATHER ANDRE: Our work is a work of glorification. Spreading one's faith is the best means of affirming it. You are trying to preserve it like the one who surrounds a flame with his two hands so that it doesn't go out. This is not the way that God wants to be worshipped (*in spite of himself, he raises his voice*). Faith only grows in those who take communion.

GERARD: But I think of all these strengths expended in vain; strength is something so precious!

FATHER ANDRE: Many seeds are lost and rot for the one which takes root. Nature confusedly symbolizes the truths that only revelation has the

ability to uncover for us; but afterwards it becomes clear in the light of revelation, which illustrates it so to speak. Have you ever thought of that axiom
of physics: "Nothing is lost, nothing is created"? Don't you see what unexpected meaning it takes when one transports it into the world of the spirit?
"Nothing is created" because all is predetermined by divine decree, "nothing
is lost" because there is not one spiritual value that is destroyed, not one of
our acts which doesn't contribute in some unforeseen way to the eternal
work.

GERARD: There is no thought that exalts me more. Not a gesture, not a
word that does not have its divine meaning, that doesn't have its place in
the universal tragedy and has not been summoned by other gestures and
other replies. My reason bows before the mystery in which it participates.

FRANCES: You hear these ramblings?

MRS. THOURET: I admit to not understanding his meaning.

FRANCES: Every evening I hear this kind of dissertation. It's generally
at the close of day; his eyes become vague, he ceases paying attention to
what I am saying; and he starts to talk, heedless ...

MRS. THOURET: To your annoyance?

FRANCES: It's not annoyance.

MRS. THOURET: Aggravation, then.

FRANCES: No, no, it's a profound anguish, a kind of inexplicable humiliation ... sometimes it resembles hatred (*speaking as if to herself*). And that
I do not understand. Because I know that the sanctuary from which I am
excluded is empty, and I laugh at the religion that is celebrated there. So
then why suffer like an exile?

MRS. THOURET: My poor child, I am not able to tell you anything to
console you. Your distress is not of those that we know, we others.

FRANCES: I know what you are going to tell me: "He will get well no doubt, he's a good husband, he will not cheat on you. Accept your lot." Such resignation, your Christian mothers have been able to communicate to you, to you who believed; but me, what example may I follow? I have broken with the ties that still bind you; the tradition to which you remain the unconscious or resigned slave means nothing to me any longer ... No, do not try to blind me, I would despise myself if I did not suffer from the conflict of our two consciences.

MRS. THOURET: You know how to be complicated and to not see life simply, like others.

FRANCES: Don't talk about those who see life simply; they are the ones who have never reflected, the ones who have never understood, those who have never defended. Slaves of their senses or their education, honest or depraved, those women will only ever be a flock—and I despise the one who is incapable of justifying her life for herself and who hasn't wanted to do so.

MRS. THOURET: My little one, all my tenderness goes out to you but it is powerless and your suffering is foreign to it.

FRANCES: It's not tenderness that I need ... I don't know myself what I'm missing; a confirmation perhaps. But, no, I don't want to be the one who bends and who looks for support. I know too well where this weakness leads.

FATHER ANDRE: (to Gerard) You will know doubt; there are hours when you'll say to yourself with terror: Can I really be chosen, me among so many others, and me instead of any of them?

GERARD: This anguish, do you think I haven't known it? But soon the anxiety becomes silent; and I hear again the continuous murmur of my happiness.

FRANCES: Ah! Isn't it awful, this happiness that he has kept for himself alone and of which I would never have my share?

MRS. THOURET: My poor child, you are perhaps only jealous!

FRANCES: Jealous of God! (*listening*) They are talking about me.

GERARD: No, I don't feel in me this power that you speak of.

FATHER ANDRE: Only He can touch the hardened heart. Perhaps one day he will send the grace to enlighten her. Our limited vision cannot penetrate the designs of God.

FRANCES: (*intending to be overheard*) Whatever surprises the future may hold for me there will be nothing in my destiny that my nature doesn't explain and that my reason doesn't justify.

FATHER ANDRE: (*with solemnity*) God alone explains and God alone justifies. (*Getting up.*) It's getting late. I'll have to leave you, my child.

GERARD: We'll not see each other again in this world.

FATHER ANDRE: (*embracing him*) My son, we will meet each other on the other side of death. (*He leaves after having acknowledged Frances, and her mother.*)

Act Three: Scene Two

The same characters, except for Father Andre

GERARD: (*at half-voice*) It seems as though I consider life like those who are no longer alive. My God! Preserve me from the vertigo of the beyond!

MRS. THOURET: (*approaching, tears in her eyes*) Gerard, my son!

GERARD: Mother, why this anxious face and this altered voice? You came to me with a heart full of pity and hands full of consolation, and now you've found joy seated at my bedside.

MRS. THOURET: (*with reproach, indicating Frances*) Joy, when …

FRANCES: Shush! You must not …

MRS. THOURET: Don't you suffer?

GERARD: The illness came to me this time like a stranger with a familiar face, like an old friend gone missing since early childhood. Who would hesitate to recognize me and would approach however with a solemn smile charged with meaning; she speaks of what has happened and asks news of those who are no longer; each of her questions is a painful wound which somehow has its secret sweetness. Do you know it, this confidential voice of illness? ... One would say that you don't understand me.

MRS. THOURET: It's true, Gerard, I do not understand you ... you don't look bad tonight, I see.

FRANCES: He isn't reasonable, he gets excited, and he doesn't listen to Doctor Schwoller, who doesn't really exert any authority over anyone and does not inspire me with confidence. Gerard should be doing better than he is.

GERARD: What do you know about it? I am doing as I should be doing.

FRANCES: (to her mother) You hear him? He has the fatalism of those who do not want to get well.

MRS. THOURET: That's bad, Gerard. For her sake, you ought to get better as soon as possible.

FRANCES: (*to her mother*) You do not think it would be worth consulting Chauvin for example? Or another?

MRS. THOURET: But is the return to Paris appropriate? Wouldn't it be serious recklessness?

Act Three: Scene Three

The same characters; Du Ryer, Marianne

MRS. THOURET: What a surprise! I didn't know you were in Montana.

Gabriel Marcel

MARIANNE: My husband is overworked and had to request a leave.

FRANCES: I thought I wrote to you about it, Mama.

MARIANNE: What do you think of his appearance?

DU RYER: Come on now, Marianne; you're not asking how Mr. Launoy is doing.

FRANCES: There's been no change for two days, I thank you.

GERARD: I am doing as well as possible. (*He coughs; Frances looks at her mother.*)

FRANCES: Mr. Du Ryer does not look too sick, it seems to me.

MARIANNE: I am not pleased with his appetite.

DU RYER: That doesn't interest anyone. (*Protestations*) (*to Mrs. Thouret*) You've had a good trip? The journey is long and tiring, isn't it?

MARIANNE: (*to Frances*) We came to ask you if you would like to do some sledding with us tomorrow afternoon?

FRANCES: Thank you, it's very kind of you.

MRS. THOURET: Isn't it a little dangerous?

FRANCES: Don't worry, mama. What time would be suitable?

MARIANNE: If you like, at three o'clock, in the shed at the top of the track. (*to Mrs. Thouret*) Have no fear, dear madam, Philip drives very well.

GERARD: Thank you for trying to distract her; she stays beside me all day long and her life is not very cheerful.

{91}

DU RYER: (*to Frances*) Have I told you that in coming, we met on the train that singular and paradoxical young man that I saw at your place?

FRANCES: Charles. Morin? What's become of him?

DU RYER: He is preparing a study on the Giotto of the Arena. But tell me, what are his philosophical ideas, in essence?

FRANCES: We know, above all, those ideas that he is fighting against. He, himself, no doubt would not be able to inform you.

DU RYER: For my part, I hardly like that skepticism, it is a social disintegrator.

MARIANNE: I found him too ironic. Why come to speak badly of the pastor? He's surely a man of great merit; he has made a great career; to think that he was only three years in Caen, two in Bordeaux, and that he came to Paris soon afterward! Isn't it one of his nephews who is going to marry Miss Antoinette: Raymond? It's a love match, is it not?

FRANCES: It is an arranged marriage, but successful. (*A brief silence.*)

MARIANNE: The other day I thought I needed to go back to Paris. Mama wrote me that my oldest had given himself indigestion. Julien is a child who eats too much when he is not supervised. (*She continues.*)

FRANCES: (*to Du Ryer, at half-voice*) I reread yesterday your Introduction to *The Psychology of Mysticism* with an emotion that you will perhaps understand one day. Nowhere have you ever shown such vigor of thought.

DU RYER: It is a book written in my youth; there are many imprudent generalizations perhaps.

MARIANNE: (*to Mrs. Thouret*) You do not know how my husband is with the children. On Sundays they behave crazily together.

FRANCES: It's true?

MARIANNE: They play hide and seek.

FRANCES: I do not see you as Henry IV, on all fours on the carpet.

DU RYER: (*excusing himself*) I cannot work all the same; they shout so loud that they give me a headache.

MRS. THOURET: (*to Frances, in a low voice*) My poor Frances, in my opinion there it is, the real tragedy of your life; those shouts of children, perhaps you will never hear them around you.

DU RYER: I would like to talk to you again someday about the Introduction. You know how important your feedback is for me with regard to what I do.

MARIANNE: Philip, I think that we would do well to return. You must not go to bed late. (*Du Ryer rises.*)

FRANCES: You are obedient.

MARIANNE: It's very important that he rest (*she helps him put on his scarf*).

FRANCES: Is there a dance at the Palace this evening?

MARIANNE: Yes, three days a week.

FRANCES: If I may, I'd like to walk a little with you. It is stifling here (*to her mother*): If I don't come back, it's because the dance will have tempted me (*going out with the Du Ryer*). Is it true that at the Palace there is an Englishman for whom all the ladies are mad?

Act Three: Scene Four

Gerard, Mrs. Thouret

MRS. THOURET: Frances is nervous tonight.

GERARD: Ah! Do you think so?

MRS. THOURET: I think that she finds you quite distant, quite strange, indifferent perhaps.

GERARD: She doesn't know then how much I am praying for her!

MRS. THOURET: It seems to me that some tender words would touch her even more.

GERARD: It's not a question of touching her ... but alas! Does she misunderstand the depth of my love? Does she bear a grudge against me, blame me for loving her more, more purely than before?

MRS. THOURET: (*with timidity*) No doubt she wonders if it is still her that you love.

GERARD: If it is she! Can she doubt it? But she doesn't know herself. Even her sacrifice has not enlightened her.

MRS. THOURET: Why are you always talking about her sacrifice? My poor child, quite simply, she loves you, she gave herself to you, she has given you her life.

GERARD: Mother, you do not know all; the act by which she accepted everything, by which she renounced herself, while there was still time, that act you are not aware of.

MRS. THOURET: What do you mean?

GERARD: The words that she pronounced, each day I have said them to myself over again, But the One who possessed her is yet an unknown to her.

MRS. THOURET: I don't understand.

GERARD: But one day you will know everything; when the act will have borne its fruit ... Dear Frances! My God, teach me words that reassure. Pardon me if I have forgotten sometimes that I still live among men, that no more than she, I am not yet liberated. (*to Mrs. Thouret*) I'll clarify things with her.

MRS. THOURET: I don't believe in the value of those explanations; the misunderstanding that separates you is not one that words can erase.

GERARD: There is no misunderstanding; if it is not known, I, I know it.

Act Three: Scene Five

The same characters; Frances

FRANCES: You cannot imagine what they have just told me; Mrs. Auriol has just taken a lover, at last! Truth be told, what astonishes me is that she has taken so long.

MRS. THOURET: Her husband is considered a very honest man.

FRANCES: He's a nincompoop.

GERARD: (*after having watched his wife*) What does it matter what happens to those people? The forces that guide them are as incomprehensible to us as those that govern matter.

FRANCES: She hasn't chosen badly; little Mark Berthet.

MRS. THOURET: (*embarrassed*) Have I told you that Mrs. Berthet is asking me to promote children's summer camps?

FRANCES: You've never seen Mark? He's nice.

MRS. THOURET: His mother must be very unhappy.

FRANCES: She's surely flattered ... an elegant woman; and as for the husband there is nothing to worry about. He's one of those who suspect nothing ... That pleased me, that story.

MRS. THOURET: I'm going to bed ... You're staying?

FRANCES: Gerard would do well to go up too.

GERARD: (*firmly*) My darling, I'd like to chat a little with you this evening.
FRANCES: You've noticed that I exist? Good, I'm listening. (*Mrs. Thouret goes out.*)

Act Three: Scene Six

Gerard, Frances

GERARD: Come a little closer, would you?

FRANCES: (*coming closer*) Is right here good?

GERARD: Sit down now. (*She sits down; a silence.*)

FRANCES: You're not saying anything?

GERARD: This ballroom music ... (*The Merry Widow Waltz is heard*).

FRANCES: What do you want? Life does not select the accompaniments. You would prefer some Bach; I would prefer silence; they give us the Merry Widow. (*With irony*) All that might have a meaning ... since everything has a meaning.

GERARD: (*with effort*) Frances, I would like you to open your heart to me tonight, as I am going to open mine to you.

FRANCES: So I have a heart?

GERARD: What I feared could be true then? You attribute to me an indescribable contempt ... when I only have tenderness for you ... and gratitude.

FRANCES: Withdraw gratitude, please.

GERARD: But it's still true! (*After a silence.*) I pity you, my dear one.

FRANCES: For not having been enlightened? I know. Spare me the education.

GERARD: Perhaps I didn't take enough care of your solitude ... perhaps I've neglected you too much! (*Strongly*) And yet no, that is not true. You are never far from my thoughts.

FRANCES: Are you sure that it's me in your thoughts?

GERARD: (*without answering*) This evening I sense you nervous and irritable, without my understanding why. Those Du Ryers perhaps ... but I don't wish to speak badly about them; they are going to try to entertain you; I am happy about that. Your existence by my side is melancholy.

FRANCES: Yes, at last I need a bit of recreation?

GERARD: Why take offense at what I am saying? Sincerely, I'm glad that these people ...

FRANCES: Why "these people"? She is a goose, I'll concede you that, but he's been the master (*eyes gleaming*), the master of my thoughts.

GERARD: The master! There are words that one must not desecrate. I seem to recall that at our wedding you did not make much of his science.

FRANCES: Then I was rich and disdain came easy to me. Today it's no longer the same. (*Quizzical look by Gerard*). Besides, it doesn't matter. It's better not to evoke the past.

GERARD: You're right … The past is only revealed in the light of the future. Needless to stir the ashes.

FRANCES: You didn't understand me. I wanted to say that good memories, one mustn't only consider on important occasions, like jewels that one draws out of cabinets for the holidays. (*after a silence, provocatively*). You must do me this justice that I never by indiscreet evocations helped to awaken your remorse.

GERARD: What remorse! I don't know if I understand you.

FRANCES: (*with a cruel smile*) You have not always been a saint, even with me.

GERARD: (*with force*) Do you think that I need you to remember what I was before? Don't I know that without your sacrifice my sins no doubt could not have been remitted? The reversibility …

FRANCES: Another pretty invention. Well then, in your opinion, you benefit from my sacrifice? That is the payoff. Let me congratulate you. They have fixed things up nicely up there, and it seems that up there they were holding on to it mightily for you to be saved.

GERARD: Spare me your irony, Frances, your words hurt me. I measure only too clearly the distance that separates you from the goal.

FRANCES: If you hold so strongly to the desire to see me "saved," I suppose it's in the hope that I will go bury myself in some obscure convent, so that you might, you also …

GERARD: Why do you keep trying to hurt me?

FRANCES: Well then, I do not understand. What interest can my salvation possibly represent? Your idea is decidedly funny (*with forced intonation*). She sacrificed, he will go to heaven … She sacrificed, he will go to heaven …

GERARD: Stop, I beg you. I doubt that it's true when you say it.

FRANCES: You doubt? Well, well … She sacrificed … That, I suppose, is divine justice!

GERARD: God is beyond justice.

FRANCES: Naturally. Justice is for imbeciles. She sacrif … Ah! Well, I've had enough. Let's come back down to earth.

GERARD: (*painfully*) Here we are.

FRANCES: Me too, I have things to say (*all the same she hesitates with difficulty on the threshold of a definitive confession*).

GERARD: What is it? (*He closes his eyes to listen.*)

FRANCES: (*she has risen and walks, a prey to an intense emotion; she looks at him, and says to herself.*) How weak he looks!

GERARD: (*indistinctly*) Well?

FRANCES: (*with great effort*) No, I won't tell you anything (*she sits down again*).

GERARD: My poor dear, revolt mounts up from the bottom of your heart only to calm itself and then rise up again. One day peace will come.

FRANCES: Alas! It will come, the peace of nothingness, without my having told anything about my passion and my despair. Which of us will disappear before the other? I don't know.

GERARD: You are not yet ready for death.

FRANCES: I'll have been a coward to the end.

GERARD: Coward? How so?

FRANCES: And this unfaithful image of me that you would keep! I see you growing more touched by my sacrifice and praying for my salvation ... It is in my power that it does not come to pass ... (*with a dark joy*). I cannot hold back.

GERARD: (*with a gesture of terror*) I do not wish ...

FRANCES: You cannot dismiss what must happen ... in five minutes we will still be here (*with a gesture*) *and* nothing will have changed ... but I will be delivered. Gerard! (*with a strange solemnity, without looking at him*), you have never understood me, I have not sacrificed myself (*with insistence*): I loved you ...

GERARD: My dearest, do you believe that you are teaching me anything? You have renounced yourself for me.

FRANCES: No, it's not for you that I madly threw myself into your arms; it's not for you, in order to save you from despair, that I did not delay a senseless marriage. It was for me—I loved you.

GERARD: Your happiness and mine were but one; they blended then, and you only differentiate them now.

FRANCES: (*with pain*) Have you never loved then, that you understand me so poorly, and even then what I was feeling for you was it truly so foreign? I will have always abused myself (*she cries*).

GERARD: (*with fright*) What? Would that be the secret of your pitiful life?

FRANCES: Gerard, I loved you. The moment I saw you, I became mad for you, your image possessed me. Oh! That delicious, that cruel obsession of you at first, when the sight of a gesture pursued me all day long. There is nothing about you, nothing about your body that did not make me dream (*a silence*) ... You see, Gerard: for years I imagined that I would take a lover.

You have been that lover. I married you, but what does that change? Yes, I have loved you well, and I don't know what you others, the saints, what you think of this love, but I assure you that it has its price, and that there are moments at home, when we were alone, on the Rue des Vignes, where I would have died without complaining ... Only life continues all the same, and we would like more, always more. (*With a gesture of infinite misery.*) Those joys should perhaps suffice for a lifetime ... but the heart is too demanding ... I have wept for them, those joys of former times, I have hoped that they be reborn, and I am not consoled ... And then this sacrifice! My God, it's quite simple: I had the desire for you, I have not been yours, I would have ... (*drawing to herself the head of Gerard*). The theory is demolished, my poor dear! (*She turns his head to look at him.*)

GERARD: (*pushing her away*) Let go ...

FRANCES: Did I hurt you? (*He nods yes.*) Finished the walk in the blue skies? Reality is not pretty ... but it is worth more than intoxicating oneself with chimeras.

GERARD: It's not for you to have mercy.

FRANCES: If you only knew how much it hurt to always lie, to never dare to be myself! I saw take root, I saw grow an awful misunderstanding ... and then you fell ill. I had to save you from a revelation that would bring you down.

GERARD: You have no need to explain ... A few words were enough for me to understand everything (*looking at her*). What misery! A shadow among shadows!

FRANCES: What do you mean?

GERARD: (*with humanity*) Memories come back to me which join together with and confirm your confession. Poor woman!

FRANCES: (*vaguely worried*) I don't want your pity.

GERARD: So from the beginning, a dark destiny was forcing you to lie ...

FRANCES: For a long time I didn't think it necessary to explain to you how I loved you.

GERARD: Willingly you concealed it.

FRANCES: There is in your words a hidden meaning that I cannot penetrate.

GERARD: I remember one of your sentences: love is a force of nature like the others.

FRANCES: Well?

GERARD: A force of nature! ... Yes, truly of nature, nothing more.

FRANCES: Don't think I've acted blindly. I chose.

GERARD: (*with a painful irony*) Chose! The eternal illusion of those who are not free!

FRANCES: (*hurt*) So have you the right to speak of illusion, you who ... and then free, have you been more so than I? Whatever be the forces that ruled your destiny ...

GERARD: To be free, it's to live in God and to collaborate in His work. What I called your sacrifice seemed to me to be the apprenticeship of that liberty which is a grace. Now I know.

FRANCES: What do you know?

GERARD: No, what good is talk? And so you loved me ... in a way? I inspired in you ... that passion? And now ...

FRANCES: I want to understand you.

GERARD: I have hurt you enough without meaning to. I can no longer give anything that you were expecting from me ... and this sad, sad life for your poor heart starving for happiness!

FRANCES: Why, Gerard, do you speak to me in that voice so changed? And why pity me so? One would say it's a child you have before you.

GERARD: Yes, an irresponsible child. (*With fervor.*) My God, she has accomplished the task that you have given her dark soul. Mechanically she has done what has needed to be done ... like a sleepwalker, like one hypnotized ... Will you awaken her one day from her sleep?

FRANCES: (*crying out*) Ah! Now I've understood! Why did I speak if nothing is changed?

GERARD: What were you hoping for?

FRANCES: Alas! He knows everything and his dream remains standing. So I would only have been an instrument!

GERARD: Nothing but an instrument.

FRANCES: I am nothing more than a thing in your eyes (*vague gesture of Gerard*). But it's just that you haven't yet understood! (*with effort*) I was not among those who give of themselves without thinking and get swept away on the wave of their passion; I have not been the sensual fool who sees nothing beyond her desire and is its plaything. If I yielded, it is because to my mind nothing is stronger than desire, and more legitimate; it's that I haven't wanted to kneel before the old idols. I justified myself.

GERARD: Justified! Passion is clever in justifying itself. I remember ... me too, in the past... Francis, I went through the same mistakes, and I have pity for you.

FRANCES: Once again, I don't want any compassion: who are you then to pity me! (*Wildly*) Ah! This atrocious thought ... So you believe this absurd thing! (*She laughs*) But all my life had prepared me for this love, it has only been the divine flowering of it. And you want that the goal of all that might only be ... your salvation? I would only have existed for you! And in what way, if you please, was your salvation of more importance than mine? ... But I don't know why I'm taking the time to reason. One doesn't argue with an invalid. (*with an artificial sweetness*). I will say nothing more.

GERARD: I want to go upstairs ... all of this has tired me. It must be late (*he painfully gets ready to rise*). Are you coming with me?

FRANCES: No, wait ... Ah! I do not want to remain alone with my thoughts.

GERARD: What more would you like to say!

FRANCES: Don't adopt this smile of the martyr. I can no longer stand it. As if I didn't know, (*with irony*) that your saintliness is only the result of your illness! (*With animation*) As if I didn't know that all this mysticism is only the protest of a soul that cannot resign itself to disappear ... It's perhaps cruel to say all this to you but I can no longer hold back. When you no longer had the strength to love ... as a man, you began to love ... as a saint. One does what one can (*she looks at him; he does not flinch*). Do you think that I haven't followed the progressions of your enlightenment, and that I might not have noticed that they coincided with those of your illness? Before, in the early days, when you were still yourself, you did not speak to me much of God and the afterlife ... and then I saw dawn this clarity ... it moved closer, the chimerical light which should have dispelled little by little the fears of the disease and throw on your mind, even on your gaze, I don't know what illusory influence. Progressively as you died to this life, you withdrew yourself into the depths of your kingdom, and men were no more to you than shadows appearing on the bright screen of your dream. However this world that you were building was only a pale image of our world, the real one, the only one. The mystic never divests himself entirely of what he was before and he invests in his outpourings to God the ardor of his kisses as a lover. (*a silence*) Gerard, the thoughts in which your soul delights are those which put one to sleep and which paralyze. It seems to me that if I were able to convince you … but I wouldn't know how. You will not recognize that without your illness …

GERARD: I will not follow you in your fictions. Everything holds together in reality.

FRANCES: You allow it. You force it?

GERARD: But universal order reveals itself to us through coincidences that our reason left to itself is powerless to interpret.

FRANCES: Coincidences! As if I didn't know that your disease is the cause!

GERARD: It was the instrument.

FRANCES: Do you think then that your case is the first and that specialists daily …

GERARD: (*interrupting her*) You think to attack me? All the old age of the world is in you. But I, I feel in my heart the eternal youth of faith (*he is taken by a fit of coughing; coming back, much lower volume*). I don't hold it against you; the self still does not know itself; always it takes itself as the most important, forgetting that its origin is beyond it, as is its end. You continue to reason, to talk nonsense, without fear of hurting me; you are right there in your role: and the same need that has handed you over to desire has made you the pupil of sophists.

FRANCES: You can deny science; it disdains your insults; it is above you, since it understands you and can foresee day by day the progress of your illness.

GERARD: The illness does not matter.

FRANCES: The changing game of your sensitivity, this game full of mystery for you, is only the relentless progression of causes, each of which may be named, measured, calculated.

GERARD: Nothing of all that is me, I experience this progression as a show.

FRANCES: Another illusion!

GERARD: You who denounce illusion everywhere, so where will you find the truth? And the ultimate illusion, isn't it the one which makes you probe beyond all illusions, a truth which you would not recognize if you met it? Because this truth is God Himself, and you deny God (*he stops exhausted; then with fervor*). My God, all this is happening in you, and is an episode of the drama that you have wanted and that will last until the end of time.

FRANCES: (*after a long silence*) We are only two poor beings who grope and tremble in the night. What good is it to fling ideas at each other?

GERARD: We *are* ideas.

FRANCES: Big words that resonate and that we, neither the one nor the other understand, when our story is so simple! What good is it to hurt ourselves? (*She closes her eyes.*) If the past could come again! I remember one evening when we were so happy. At Sevres, you had come to dinner, and we walked in the kitchen garden. The evening was mild; there were no stars.

GERARD: Why recall that now?

FRANCES: We sat down and you flung your arms around my neck without speaking.

GERARD: Yes, I remember. What good ...

FRANCES: (*continuing without looking at Gerard*) And I, I thought of the moment when I would belong to you entirely. I was dreaming for our union an indescribable romantic décor ...

GERARD: (*uneasily*) Those memories hurt you.

FRANCES: And all this love that I had for you would have been but a means of preparing your salvation? ... I would have always been led and my life would only have been a necessary illusion!

GERARD: Your science makes of it something else?

FRANCES: Alas! (*She cries, then slowly she exits.*)

(*Gerard left alone, pulls a book from his pocket, opens it, and begins to read; but he is distracted and lets it fall; he seems prey to some kind of conflict; he gets up, goes to the mirror, looks at himself for a long time; he passes his hand over his emaciated chest, and an expression of distress is painted on his sober face.*)

GERARD: (*in a toneless voice*) One evening ... at Sevres

CURTAIN

ACT FOUR

(*In the shed. At three o'clock in the afternoon. A single scene. Frances, Du Ryer*)

Frances enters briskly through the back door which remains ajar; one can see the snow falling in a gray day, Du Ryer goes to her.

DU RYER: My wife asked me to present her apologies; she is really sorry but at the last minute she saw that she could not come.

FRANCES: She is not ill, I hope?

DU RYER: No, no; just a little tired (*after a pause*). Should we try to do a little sledding, even though it is snowing?

FRANCES: No, thank you; if you like we can stay here instead. It's been a long time since I've talked alone with you.

DU RYER: With the greatest pleasure. We should close the door. The snow is entering right up to here (*he goes to close the door; then both sit on the only bench on the right along the wall*). Would you mind telling me just what you thought of my Introduction, on rereading it?

FRANCES: I would like to talk about something else today. Let's talk about you instead.

DU RYER: It is not a very interesting subject. I lead the monotonous and rather gray existence of all university professors. My life is mixed with my work ... Have I told you that I will found a new journal?

FRANCES: No.

DU RYER: A journal of Religious Psychology. It will be an international Review, a monthly one, published in Paris. Many important foreign writers have promised me their support. We will have correspondents almost everywhere. Today, you must realize, the essential thing is to centralize information. I would therefore like it if it were above all a compendium, a directory, as rich in facts as possible.

FRANCES: Yes ... You really believe in facts?

DU RYER: What do you mean?

FRANCES: What is a fact? Where does it begin? An illusion, a belief, are they facts?

DU RYER: Everything that is observable is a fact.

FRANCES: But can you observe a belief?

DU RYER: I understand you less and less. A belief translates into a series of experimentally seizable manifestations, outside of which it is nothing.

FRANCES: Nothing? Everything is there.

DU RYER: (*listening to himself speak*) A belief is the result of psychological forces that we are able to determine, that we perhaps one day will be able to measure. It plunges so to speak, from all sides into physics, into the observable. In itself it is ...

FRANCES: Only a belief.

DU RYER: One would say, dear madam, that there is something different about you.

FRANCES: It's possible ... after hours that I've spent ... I will remember those hours of anguish and insomnia. But it matters little. It is not about me.

DU RYER: You know how much everything that touches you interests me, however.

FRANCES: Really?

DU RYER: Can you doubt it?

FRANCES: No, I believe you (*a silence*).

DU RYER: (*just to say something*) Mr. Launoy seemed better to me last night.

FRANCES: There is not any appreciable change (*in another tone*). Tell me, Mr. Du Ryer, have you made this quite simple reflection, that the people whose stories you note with curiosity, the people known by initials, you know, whose bizarre adventures fill your books and your articles, have lived, have thought, have suffered like you, like me?

DU RYER: The direction of your questions is a puzzle for me. No doubt it might occur that the psychologist be partially duped by the plan he is using ...

FRANCES: You misunderstand me. Have you ever thought that an individual, in spite of everything, is something other than the ensemble of phenomena that you describe, that you pretend to analyze?

DU RYER: From the standpoint of experimental science, it is surely nothing more than what you say.

FRANCES: But from the standpoint of one's conscience ...

DU RYER: Your turn now dear lady, allow me a question. The problems that you pose are those that would no longer embarrass a bachelor (*ironic smile of Frances*). Admit that you have undergone an influence. I thought I noticed that Mr. Launoy ...

FRANCES: (*laughing bitterly*) Rest assured. My husband has not converted me. No, but a faith has died in me tonight and will not be replaced.

DU RYER: But explain to me, I entreat you ... Of course I have no right to a secret. But you know what you have been to me; you sense it at least.

FRANCES: No, I cannot explain. It is for you to enlighten me.

DU RYER: (*with resignation*) Speak.

FRANCES: Does science exhaust the contents of an individual or if not (*hesitating*) does it acknowledge that there remains in him … a principle which it does not understand?

DU RYER: But these are metaphysical questions that you are asking of me … I do not know … all that matters for the scientist is the observable, calculable data.

FRANCES: For the scientist so be it: for man, surely not.

DU RYER: (*with self-satisfaction*) Without doubt one cannot ask of all men to raise themselves to the level of abstraction implied by scientific research.

FRANCES: You speak of all men with a singular disdain. But we are "all men," you and I. Let's say that for two hours a week, when you exercise your priesthood there in Saint Anne (*gesture of Du Ryer*) you are feeling good … the rest of the time you are Mr. Du Ryer, and you forget them, all those notions of which you are so proud.

DU RYER: Without a doubt …

FRANCES: But if these notions were only the artificial products of a reason eager for order and clarity? For, finally, what did they give, your theories and your hypotheses?

DU RYER: They succeed.

FRANCES: At what do they succeed? Show me factual confirmations, positive applications.

DU RYER: (*with comic despair*) I was not expecting to see you, you, put psychology on trial!

FRANCES: Where you affirm the causal links, another will only see the coincidences whose reason escapes us. What experiment would settle the matter in your favor? None; you know it— and yet you claim to explain a spiritual state by an organic one.

DU RYER: Let me. I limit myself to assert a necessary relation between the facts.

FRANCES: That's it, you revel in this abstract language. What does this relationship matter if you cannot explain it? What men eternally would like to know is the why and not the how. You will be able to hide yourself well behind the limits of experimental science; but in that way you will ruin its credit.

DU RYER: Certainly when you consider things with hindsight ...

FRANCES: Let's admit it. Why would I be right then, rather than now (*wildly*) at this atrocious time when I struggle in vain against dark powers around me, in me, everywhere. Will you have the audacity to ... pardon my friend ... to come to talk to me, to me, about clear ideas, to me who am so bruised and desperate ... and to exalt before me logic and coherence? ... No, no, for this kind of impassioned expression a faith in the beautiful order of the world would be necessary, a faith that we no longer possess, neither one nor the other. God would be necessary, you see, one does not do without impunity. No, not experimental science, I beg of you; because if you claim the unknowable ... But what good does it do to argue? I tell you I am exhausted, I am at the end of my rope, I am only just a ...

DU RYER: Take care. One does not keep to these negations for a long time and all mysticisms threaten ...

FRANCES: (*with a mysterious sadness*) No, have no fear. The path that opens before me is not one of those which leads to God.

DU RYER: I do not understand you.

FRANCES: Know only that if I turn away from the illusion of science, it is not to stretch out my arms to the illusion of faith ... Your timid soul is frightened and outraged by my words. And yet, if one asked you, you, to justify your scientific faith, what would you say? (*He does not answer.*) You would be right not to answer; justifications are perhaps only ever deceptions.

DU RYER: Permit me.

FRANCES: If you were logical, you would keep from denying it. If conscience is only a shadow which follows our actions, then, far from directing them, the reasons that we give for our conduct are only a deception.

DU RYER: But why do you reproach science? I think I find behind your professions of faith an indescribable personal grievance that you are not expressing.

FRANCES: My story matters little. If you were honest you would admit that science has only been for you an entertainment, a screen placed by you between yourself and reality. Ah, the misery of your lives as scholars who laboriously weave the lie of a doctrine ... in order not to be placed in the presence of destiny ... Yes, my friend, there the big word is spoken. Destiny! I believe that we are the playthings of some incomprehensible power that leads us. This is not new and it is discouraging ... I think that reason is an illusion, vital if you wish, which has no other goal but to hide from us our powerlessness and our fragility. All the wisdom to which we can claim is to understand that all is an illusion. The truth is still illusion but illusion is not fooled by itself.

DU RYER: Then where do you find it, this truth?

FRANCES: Must I tell you?

DU RYER: Yes.

FRANCES: It is in the desire that accepts itself as misleading and as ephemeral; in the desire that seeks no false justifications; it is ... But what good is all this? Isn't it for you to answer and to demonstrate (*with irony*), for you who are a master?

DU RYER: (*sadly*) There is nothing in what you have said that I haven't heard and refuted a hundred times; how is it that these words upset me when it is you who pronounce them? (*a silence*) It's that you have been my pupil, the one in whom I have seen awaken the passion for truth ... I recall some conversations that we have had previously. More than I, you had that scientific faith that now ...

FRANCES: Your teaching has not stood the test of life, doubtless because it wasn't based in life. Science is inefficacious when it is not wisdom. So who were you to talk about mystics, you, an atheist?

DU RYER: We really only understand that which we do not feel. Objectivity ...

FRANCES: Again the big words. Admit it: the project of science is not that of life. As long as you speculate on gravity or electricity, you have the right to reason about symbols and fictions; but when you claim to reconstruct the hidden work of souls, ah! That's when the danger begins.

DU RYER: Do you think that I cannot guess the misunderstandings from which you emerged wounded, discouraged, hopeless? No doubt you were not sufficiently armed for the struggle which you have had to bear.

FRANCES: Let it suffice me to have resisted the contagion of faith. You may well despise me.

DU RYER: Me, despise you? No, no, and if I regret to see lost to our cause the strength of your intelligence ... (*Frances gives a wry smile*). Why are you laughing? You have never understood how much I admired you.

FRANCES: I was the good hard-working pupil, enthusiastic even, and who occasionally restores confidence to the discouraged master. Alright, perhaps I have been like that.

DU RYER: You have been more than that.

FRANCES: No, for you have never ... (*she stops herself*). Now that I no longer work by your side, I no longer exist for you.

DU RYER: What do you know?

FRANCES: Don't get excited. If you had ever felt for me more than that complacent esteem in which there is vanity, - I was your student—you would have suspected ...

DU RYER: Here you are stopping again. Why?

FRANCES: My poor friend, if you could see what a funny face you are making right now! You have the puzzled look of a child who doesn't know if he wants to or if he is afraid to know.

DU RYER: Do not stop on the threshold of ...

FRANCES: You were going to say the confession; why not the declaration while you're at it? You do not lack conceit!

DU RYER: Have pity on me. You cannot know whether by these single hesitations you have already done me much harm.

FRANCES: Tell me outright, after all, what you suppose! Do you believe in good faith that I loved you?

DU RYER: (*simply*) Yes.

FRANCES: Well, well, it's true. Don't say anything, you will spoil your yes, it was the "yes" of a child.

DU RYER: (*at half-voice*) I feel a giddiness at the thought of what might have been.

FRANCES: Nothing could have happened: you were married (*a silence*).

DU RYER: You are playing horribly with me, it's not possible. It is only more cruelty.

FRANCES: There are truths that do hurt. You cannot know what you have inspired in me. If I told you certain details ...

DU RYER: (*childishly*) Don't tell them.

FRANCES: When I went to my aunt's house, I remember, I used to take a detour to pass by your house, and then ... (*changing tone*). To sum it all up, it is only the first love of a schoolgirl for her teacher. A known phenomenon you know, and among the most common. There is nothing in this little tale that deserves your attention (*with irony*), if it's not that you've been the hero of it.

DU RYER: My God, what interest do you have in telling me all this now?

FRANCES: Not very good for a psychologist! You don't understand that there are experiences which tempt?

DU RYER: (*sadly*) Then I was right, it was not true.

FRANCES: You are tiresome. I tell you that nothing is more true; ask my friend Antoinette.

DU RYER: You have told her!

FRANCES: And then again, what is it that that could do to you, the past as far past as all that? (*With intended kindness*) Let's see now, you're not going to give yourself ideas, hypnotize yourself over this poor episode, you, a happy man, a reasonable man, a scholar! (*Du Ryer has a movement of impatience.*) I could not have been the only one, you know, the little Aubier girl ...

DU RYER: Only one thing consoles me; you will find me terribly ridiculous, if I say it.

FRANCES: Say it anyway.

DU RYER: Uh, well, it seems to me that if I had become totally indifferent to you, you would not have told me about it (*taking hold of himself again*); that is ...

FRANCES: Too late, my friend, you have blundered irreparably. (*Harshly*) But don't you see that one could give my avowal another interpretation, a little less favorable to your self-esteem?

DU RYER: I do not understand you.

FRANCES: Think about it. There is some presumption on your part in attributing to a residue of love what can also be due to ... (*she stops*). Needless to explain to you after all. You would always be free to not believe me.

DU RYER: One would say that the dire need to inflict pain possesses you at this time. You do not know yourself what your real thoughts are, and you are collecting like stones all the words which hurt to throw in my face ... And yet I think that I read you. You've come here with the intention to ridicule me, and this fever that you are igniting in me, you only fuel in order to mock me. I can see clearly now and I am suffering. You've achieved your purposes, you have made of me what you wanted. It seems that you've killed in me all strength and all certainty.

FRANCES: It grows back very quickly, certainty, you will see; and then you will only need three hours of it a week.

DU RYER: Do not pretend not to understand me. It is no longer a question of our ideas, it is a question of ourselves. I love you, and I hate you, I ...

FRANCES: (*with solemnity*) My friend, do you see at last that from all these remarks, that from all these clouds which were separating us, a kind of clearing has opened? It is very humble, alas! Let us however humiliate ourselves before it. This obscure appetite that I read in you— if you knew how your eyes have changed within an hour!—this type of childish prestige with which your ingenuousness dresses you at this moment, all that is ephemeral, all that is mediocre, but all that is true. Your presumption and your science are like broken toys. There are no longer present but two per-ishable bodies that covet each other and that call each other. My friend, let us have at least the frightful courage of knowing that we are just that, the courage to dare to be just that. We will not back down, you feel it as I do. Before entering into this shadow which solicits us, we owe it to ourselves to illuminate this moment. I have come to bring you one last light. Have you considered well?

DU RYER: (*in a low voice*) Yes.

FRANCES: There is then no more to do but to put out the light. And now ... (*She stands up*).

DU RYER: When will I see you again, Frances? (*Frances makes vague gesture.*) Do you love me?

FRANCES: You mustn't question anymore. I told you that the light was out.

CURTAIN

ACT FIVE

In Paris, at the home of the Launoys, same décor as in the second act. A day in Spring; it is five o'clock.

Act Five: Scene One

Gerard; then Oliver

As the curtain goes up, Gerard is alone; he is seated in an armchair and is looking at a photograph. Tea has been served; the side table has not yet been cleared. The door opens, Gerard precipitously places the photograph back on the table.

GERARD: Hello, Oliver. Are you back from the station?

OLIVER: Yes, but it's necessary that I speak to Frances. Where is she?

GERARD: In her room, with her mother and Miss Raymond. I think that she is trying on a hat. Sit down and let's chat awhile (*he gives Oliver an affectionate look*).

OLIVER: (*pulling out his watch*) Yes, I have the time. Do you know that I find you very changed? You have regained some color, you no longer have drawn features; even your voice is no longer the same.

GERARD: (*with emotion*) Is it true?

OLIVER: And this change must have been very rapid; because the letter written by mum the evening of her arrival in Montana was radiating discouragement. Since then it's been less than two months.

GERARD: Only six weeks.

OLIVER: And how do you feel today?

GERARD: Around the middle of the day, I am really good. It seemed at the last check-up that my heart gave the doctor some concern, but it should be nothing.

OLIVER: You no longer have a temperature, even in the evening?

GERARD: No, not for fifteen days.

OLIVER: I only regret that you didn't stay there several weeks more, for it is surely the effect of the stay that is showing now.

GERARD: We were not able to stay longer; the thaw was approaching; and then you have no idea of the dreariness of this country. Never this life of light that I love so much, and of which she has such great need.

OLIVER: (*surprised*) Frances?

GERARD: She was suffering from that sinister nature out there.

OLIVER: I thought however that the sunshine of the mountain tops ...

GERARD: No, no; it's in the south only that the light is joyful and revives. The south! ... There I will recover completely.

OLIVER: Gerard, I am so happy to see you finally aspire to health; this is for me the best of symptoms, this momentum toward recovery. In the past, while admiring your serenity, I used to suffer to see you so resigned ... You smile strangely: why?

GERARD: Let's not speak of past times ... I am happy that you are beside me, Oliver. You will come to see us there, isn't that right? On vacation?

OLIVER: Yes, I will do my best in order to come be with you.

GERARD: I look at you with all my soul ... Who knows? If destiny wished that I might not see you again! ... What sweetness and what faith in your eyes!

OLIVER: Alas! You know it, I don't have any faith. That I don't have your certainties? Mum spoke to me of that missionary that you met out there.

GERARD: An admirable man. You would have liked him. He told me many a profound thing, and you saw his life behind each one of his words (*a silence*). That is so far away already!

OLIVER: Gerard, I would like to believe and I cannot. If I am going to come see you, will you allow me to tell you my doubts?

GERARD: I am not among those who know how to answer ... Don't turn your anxious face to me (*with trouble*); others are more worthy than I of your confidence and your respect.

OLIVER: No, no.

GERARD: My soul is less pure than you think (*a silence; he looks at Oliver*). Do you know that you have changed as well? (*in a half-voice*) Tell me, is there nothing new in your life? ...

OLIVER: (*to divert the conversation*) Say, this photograph of you? It wasn't here before.

GERARD: (*with embarrassment*) Your mother has lost the old one; I will give her this one shortly (*a silence; Oliver goes to the window and looks out*). Come close to me. I am not able yet to speak so strongly. (*Oliver moves closer.*) Well, you don't want to tell me about yourself?

OLIVER: It's just that there is nothing to say.

GERARD: You are at the age when it seems as though there is nothing happening; and yet it's when all is stirring?

OLIVER: My work takes practically all of my time.

GERARD: Ah?

OLIVER: It should not be of interest to you.

GERARD: Why?

OLIVER: It seems as though you live so far removed from all of that!

GERARD: (*with emotion*) No man can remain in the eternal.

OLIVER: You didn't speak like that before.

GERARD: It's true. Back then I didn't foresee ...

OLIVER: What do you mean?

GERARD: Better that you don't understand (*a silence*). Oliver, are you chaste?

OLIVER: (*blushing, in a half-voice*) You well know it.

GERARD: I love you thus.

OLIVER: I don't understand the emotion that is in your heart. In the past ...

GERARD: Yes, in the past ...

Act Five: Scene Two

The same characters; Frances, Antoinette, Mrs. Thouret

FRANCES: (*to Oliver*) Hello, I didn't know that you were here, Oliver. Well! The tickets?

OLIVER: There are no longer seats left on the express train on Saturday; but there are some on Sunday's train. I wanted to consult you before reserving.

FRANCES: I guess we will have to resign ourselves to a day's delay then.

MRS. THOURET: You are not a day away.

OLIVER: I'll go right now to reserve the seats.

FRANCES: First have a cup of tea; I'm sure that Gerard didn't think to offer you something. And then you're coming to dinner, don't forget. Antoinette will not be with us because the annoying individual to whom she is about to give her hand ...

ANTOINETTE: I'm telling you, please don't mind ...

OLIVER: Let it be: you're delighted that we're picking on him in front of you.

ANTOINETTE: My feelings are not your concern.

MRS. THOURET: Your fiancé delights me; we chatted the entire evening, the day before yesterday.

ANTOINETTE: If you spoke to him about investments, it doesn't surprise me.

MRS. THOURET: I think he has very reasonable ideas about life; he has a sense of the responsibilities that weigh on a young household.

ANTOINETTE: (*fearfully*) To that point!

MRS. THOURET: He's not one of those who throw themselves into marriage without reflection, and then go to a marriage counselor.

FRANCES: We know that Antoinette is making a marriage of expedience. We do not need to remind her about it again.

MRS. THOURET: Marriages of reason ...

FRANCES: Mother, are you going to repeat that they are the only ones which succeed?

ANTOINETTE: What! You condescend to take part in such disrespectful discussion? I am not at all grateful for your participation; for if you are predicting divorce for me at the end of six months ...

MRS. THOURET: It's dreadful that there are divorces now!

GERARD: (to Antoinette) For me to be able to predict divorce for you, it would first be necessary for me to see that your marriage existed.

ANTOINETTE: And why doesn't it exist? Is it for lack of ecclesiastical benediction?

GERARD: What my mother-in-law calls a "marriage of reason" (all rationale and no emotion) is not a marriage for me.

ANTOINETTE: (with a threatening gesture) You're not going to talk to us about the mystical union of souls!

GERARD: (with sadness) No, I will not oppose you with the example of those who do not even want to be praised by our profane mouths (Oliver raises his head and looks at him sadly). The carnal desire of two creatures who are burning to belong to one another is still perhaps a justification.

ANTOINETTE: (to Frances) Well then, Frances, your husband is becoming more human, it seems.

FRANCES: (whose discomfort is visible) I didn't notice.

GERARD: (to Antoinette) Make no mistake about the meaning of my words. There is no carnal love which is not obscured by the shadow of another love, which is not saddened by the regret of a lost paradise.

ANTOINETTE: I recognize the old you again.

FRANCES: Let it go ...

ANTOINETTE: No, continue, it's interesting!

OLIVER: Don't you see he is ailing?

MRS. THOURET: Gerard, take care of yourself!

GERARD: But there remains hidden in the depths of the most troubled desire, the premonition of a transfiguration ... It would be too awful if for the one who has awakened in the world, there were no promise of deliverance.

ANTOINETTE: You are becoming prophetic again. What about me then, since I'm making a reasonable marriage ... (*jokingly*) it's very sad, you know. If I had suspected the revelation that awaited me here, I would not have come.

MRS. THOURET: So let it go my child. I don't understand what Gerard is talking about ... But, I can guarantee you that marriages like yours are often those which turn out the best.

ANTOINETTE: Dear Madam, you give me courage ... (*to the others*). You see, Mrs. Thouret is very hopeful.

GERARD: Why should you not be what people call happy?

ANTOINETTE: My marriage is already pretty good. I will try to be content with that.

GERARD: But when I think of all that you will not know!

OLIVER: (*laughing*) You don't know anything about it. There are happy matches.

ANTOINETTE: Go on.

OLIVER: Did I shock you?

ANTOINETTE: You wouldn't! … Well, perhaps I am going to astound you: it would bother me a great deal to cheat on my husband.

MRS. THOURET: Well, do tell now! What kind of ideas are these?

GERARD: All of that doesn't matter. The man that you marry without love, can he claim your fidelity?

ANTOINETTE: You do well, you mystics, when you get involved.

FRANCES: See here, Gerard!

MRS. THOURET: (*in a half-voice*) You know that he is transformed.

FRANCES: (*to herself*) Transformed!

MRS. THOURET: For more than six months I haven't seen him so well.

FRANCES: (*who no longer conceals her anguish*) Really!

MRS. THOURET: For me it's only a question of patience.

FRANCES: (*feeling the weight of Oliver looking at her*) Gerard! Why don't you go out a little with Oliver? You would even be able to sit down in the Luxembourg Gardens. The weather is very mild tonight.

OLIVER: (*pulling out his watch*) Indeed, perhaps it's better that I get going. The office could be closed.

GERARD: I'll accompany you (*they go out together*).

MRS. THOURET: Me too, I'm going to put on my hat. I have bridge at six o'clock with your uncle Anatole, and he doesn't allow us to be late.

She goes out.

Gabriel Marcel

Act Five: Scene Three

Frances, Antoinette

ANTOINETTE: Your husband has entertained me a lot.

FRANCES: Oh?

ANTOINETTE: Yes, I think he's softened his opinions.

FRANCES: (*awkwardly*) I never argue with him.

ANTOINETTE: And then he becomes romantic ... it's funny how you are all romantic; you put capital letters on passion, on love; I'm not speaking of your mother, of course.

FRANCES: Yes, mama ...

ANTOINETTE: It looks as though something's bothering you.

FRANCES: Absolutely nothing.

ANTOINETTE: We've hardly seen each other during your stay. I was sorry that you were not free yesterday afternoon.

FRANCES: (*briskly*) Gerard needed me; I was unable to leave him.

ANTOINETTE: Physically, he is transformed.

FRANCES: Yes.

ANTOINETTE: Perhaps this explains ...

FRANCES: It may.

ANTOINETTE: You understood me immediately.

FRANCES: It wasn't difficult.

ANTOINETTE: (*after looking at her*) You are hiding something from me aren't you?

FRANCES: (*with impatience*) How many times will it be necessary to repeat that nothing is bothering me!

ANTOINETTE: You are nervous.

FRANCES: I am tired. I had to extend myself heavily out there. And one only feels the fatigue afterward. (*Mrs. Thouret enters.*)

MRS. THOURET: I am ready. Are you accompanying me, Antoinette?

ANTOINETTE: I will stay just a few more minutes with Frances.

MRS. THOURET: (*to her daughter*) Perhaps I'll come by a little tomorrow towards five o'clock.

FRANCES: (*briskly*) No, I'll be on Vivienne Street, at the dressmaker's.

MRS. THOURET: Really, I thought she had moved.

FRANCES: Yes, that's right, I meant to say on Boulevard Malesherbes. Come instead for dinner.

MRS. THOURET: Fine. Bye bye. (*She goes out.*)

ANTOINETTE: Your mother looks good, the altitude did her some good. By the way, in Montana, you saw again your former idol (*ironically*), the professor Du Ryer?

FRANCES: Yes. I saw him very little. His wife is a simpleton. I don't understand how one marries someone like that.

ANTOINETTE: In other words, the professor Du Ryer has fallen in your esteem.

Act Five: Scene Four

The same characters; Charles Morin

CHARLES: (*after having shaken hands with Antoinette and Frances*) I knew you were passing through Paris, and I had to come for news of Mr. Launoy.

FRANCES: My husband is better, significantly better. But we are leaving again in three days.

CHARLES: I am glad to hear ...

FRANCES: And the Giottos of the Arena? It's moving ahead, your book?

CHARLES: How did you know?

FRANCES: Were you keeping it a secret?

CHARLES: Ah! I've got it. That excellent Mr. Du Ryer told you ... Mr. Du Ryer is he doing well?

FRANCES: I suppose so.

CHARLES: Fine! So much the better.

ANTOINETTE: He's still the bane of your existence?

CHARLES: But I don't wish him any harm, I'm asking you to believe it. Besides, I've only met him on two occasions, one of them here.

FRANCES: You were unbearable that day; I remember your exit on the subject of Saint Paul.

ANTOINETTE: Seriously, you think he is quite dangerous, this poor Mr. Du Ryer?

CHARLES: On no account. His doctrines will always find an antidote in common sense.

ANTOINETTE: What? You, you are extolling common sense?

CHARLES: Common sense is a passerine bird, but a very harmless passerine bird. How will you ever persuade her that there is necessarily an alternative between the visceral explanations of Mr. Du Ryer, and the most transcendent mysticism?

ANTOINETTE: I don't understand, you know.

CHARLES: God exists or He does not exist; it's very simple. But the effort of humanity, since one has been able to reason, has been to escape this dilemma: it believes it has succeeded—at the price of such contradictions! And all your pedantry will change nothing about it.

FRANCES: Do not hope to block us by your fictional dilemmas. Destinies meet and divide like waters; I do not believe in a common source from which they emanate. The scientist is free to call necessity the chance events that lead him. As for me …

CHARLES: (*to Frances*) You have come a long way. But you came back to the wisdom of men; only what you call chance, they call freedom.

ANTOINETTE: Basically all this is only a matter of words.

FRANCES: (*to Charles*) What good is it to argue? You will not convince me any more than you are convinced yourself.

CHARLES: Then you take me for a vulgar sophist?

FRANCES: For a lover of paradoxes at least.

{130}

CHARLES: But it is absolutely false; I guarantee you that the other day at the Brera, or yesterday, while I was listening to the "Enchantment of Good Friday" …

FRANCES: Yes, this is quite right.

ANTOINETTE: In any case, the things God wills, if they exist, are not those things which get certified. We therefore do not need to worry about them.

FRANCES: (*listening*) I think I hear my husband. I beg your pardon. (*She goes to the door.*) Gerard!

CHARLES: (*to Gerard, who enters*) I am happy to hear how well you are doing (he shakes his hand). I'm sorry that I cannot stay.

FRANCES: You're leaving already?

CHARLES: I must, a meeting …

FRANCES: (*to Antoinette, who gets up*) You too, you are leaving us? Stay a little longer.

ANTOINETTE: No, it is late. When will I see you again? (*She leaves with Charles and Frances.*)

Act Five: Scene Five

Frances, Gerard

(*Frances comes back after a moment and goes to Gerard, who is standing near the window.*)

FRANCES: You've come back so early! You didn't sit awhile in the Luxembourg Garden?

GERARD: No, I did not have the patience for it (*he seems to expect a question which does not come*). I accompanied Oliver a little way, and then I came back by a detour. The evening is admirable.

FRANCES: The sky was beautiful just now.

GERARD: One enjoys being alive tonight (*a silence*).

FRANCES: I think that you were wrong to walk all the time. You should lie down now. I see in your face that you're a little tired.

GERARD: (*a bit upset*) No, you're wrong.

FRANCES: With all that, you are nervous. We had people all afternoon, and I noticed that you were not managing well.

GERARD: Why are you treating me as an invalid, now that I am practically recovered?

FRANCES: You still need to take care of yourself a good bit. You shouldn't want to go so fast. (*A moment.*) I haven't given you any trouble?

GERARD: I assure you that I feel as I used to.

FRANCES: So much the better; but do not jeopardize this great result.

GERARD: (*more and more nervous*) Don't talk like that. I am no longer ill.

FRANCES: (*submissive*) All right (*a silence*).

GERARD: (*going to the piano*) Just now I was obsessed with a phrase of Debussy; do you remember? (*He searches for the theme at the piano.*)

"And the evenings on the balcony, charged with the fragrance of roses,"

And then especially what comes after, oh! That phrase:

"How sweet was your bosom for me! How good was your heart to me!"

Do you remember?

FRANCES: Yes.

GERARD: In the past, you used to sing it, I think.

FRANCES: You know very well that I no longer sing. And further—I say all the same—you are wrong to excite yourself over this music, it hurts the nerves.

GERARD: You don't feel the sweetness of this resolution? (*He repeats the phrase on the piano.*)

FRANCES: Now, make me happy: lie down a bit.

GERARD: Someone rang! (*He quickly goes to the door in the background; and speaks in a choked voice.*) Martha! Say that we are not here, neither of us!

FRANCES: (*in a low voice*) What, let's see! (*They stop talking, one hears the door of the entrance hall closing.*) Martha, who was it?

THE MAID: Mrs. Gauvin, madam.

FRANCES: Thank you (*she comes back to Gerard*). Did you hear that? It was Lucy. She will tell Mama that we were not at home, and then ... it's ridiculous; I'm going to call her back.

GERARD: (*holding her back*) No, don't go. I want to be alone with you.

FRANCES: But what will Lucy think when she finds out ... ?

GERARD: I don't care.

FRANCES: You are mad. I don't know what has come over you (*her voice changes*). You are not the same.

GERARD: (*his eyes set in a stare*) It's true, I am no longer the same.

FRANCES: (*trying to recover her composure*) You give me a lot of trouble, yes, a lot, and this nervousness cannot be a good sign.

GERARD: (*with a gesture*) Please.

FRANCES: I really regret that we're not leaving tomorrow. The air in Paris, and all these visits ...

GERARD: Don't condescend to treat me as an invalid.

FRANCES: (*with uneasiness*) What do you mean?

GERARD: Nothing more than what I am saying.

FRANCES: (*after having looked at him*) Pardon me, my darling, if I've hurt you (*she hugs him*). Do you think that I don't rejoice to see you get better?

GERARD: I know ...

FRANCES: Lie down, and I'll come sit right beside you (*he lies down on the sofa; she sits by his side, she caresses him*).

GERARD: (*happy*) Frances!

FRANCES: Don't speak. It's good? (*He puts his arm around her neck.*) Don't mess up my hair!

GERARD: I love you!

FRANCES: I really hope this is not something new; and it's not worth saying that to me in a distraught tone (*a silence*). In five minutes I'll have to go and say something to the kitchen.

GERARD: No.

FRANCES: What do you mean, no?

GERARD: Why don't you seem to understand me? Yes, why ... I love you ... as you used to love me.

FRANCES: But you are overwhelming me, my darling.

GERARD: Why do you feign astonishment? Since we've been here, there hasn't been one of my gestures, one of my looks which hasn't shown you the truth. There are signs which a woman—a woman such as yourself—does not mistake.

FRANCES: These signs. Can I be sure of understanding them well? Was such a change likely?

GERARD: You would prefer not to know it.

FRANCES: Shouldn't I have spared you painful questions or allusions, hurtful ones perhaps?

GERARD: You haven't always been so discreet. Your exceptional prudence is hard to explain.

FRANCES: What do you mean? There seems to be a reproach in your words.

GERARD: Only restlessness. No, I don't blame you for having reawakened in me the feelings that I thought were dried up ...

FRANCES: Me?

GERARD: It's you who by your confessions awakened in me the yearning for love, then love itself; it's you who, recalling what I had been for you, inspired in me the morbid desire to become a lover again ... but what good is it to explain to you? I love you, and I want you all to myself.

FRANCES: (*with fright*) So the words that I pronounced ... that night ... They've taken root in you?

GERARD: Perhaps it was only punishment for my impetuous pride. How I suffered, alas, during these few weeks!

FRANCES: Me, I did that without suspecting a thing! And at the very moment that I was crying over my defeat, I was shaking your foundations ... I remember your calm while I was crying my distress.

GERARD: There is in your voice an anguish that I don't understand. Go on, let's forget, you your humiliations and I my hopes. As you were saying that evening, we are only men and I don't know how to resist the desire that is soliciting me ... Why this fright on your face?

FRANCES: I don't know, I ...

GERARD: Come, my poor Frances, I understand only too well.

FRANCES: No, it's not that.

GERARD: You deny in vain. You had reason to close your eyes. Alas! The weeks, the months of illness!

FRANCES: No, no.

GERARD: But I love you, and I am young and strong like before (*showing the photograph*). Am I so different then than the one that you loved?

FRANCES: The old picture! (*She breaks out into sobs.*)

GERARD: Why are you crying like that? Come, I want to give you back the taste for caresses.

FRANCES: It's you who are talking like that, you ...

GERARD: I no longer have memory ... We are alone ... the past is extinguished like an illusory sky (*he passes his arm in desperation around her neck, then in a muffled voice*) ... tell me ... it's true then? I disgust you?

FRANCES: (*crying out*) No, I swear it ... (*with bewilderment*) but we can't (*she looks around her*) ... it's insane, this sudden desire.

GERARD: Sudden? It was slowly rekindled, the fever that is consuming me.

FRANCES: You cannot think of ... it would be imprudent ... if you had asked the doctor, surely. .

.

GERARD: Find some other pretext. What wears one out is desire unfulfilled. You cannot talk! Before you didn't have such fears. Then you were in love ... and then all this is absurd. I want you to tell me to my face ...

FRANCES: Then you don't see that you've conquered me again! The desire that is shaking you, it's also in me! ... Ah! Why must I lose you forever at the moment that I find you!

GERARD: What do you mean?

FRANCES: I cannot belong to you.

GERARD: Explain ... why you prohibit yourself like that?

FRANCES: It's myself that I'm prohibiting! (*Desperate*) No, do not extend to me your poor arms that in my dreams I've covered with kisses! And that look, that tempting look! (*She turns away her eyes.*)

GERARD: (*with mounting fear*) What is it that stands between us?

FRANCES: Be quiet. I can no longer hear that voice that I have loved too much.

GERARD: But what is ... what is it finally?

FRANCES: (*to herself*) Nothing more—nothing but shadow and silence.

GERARD: Frances, I can imagine everything.

FRANCES: (*slowly, with accentuation*) You can imagine everything (he gets up). I have fallen so low, I am not one of those who are shared.

GERARD: (*crying out*) Ah! You, you have ... that dishonor! (*He makes a violent gesture.*)

FRANCES: Yes, me, I have betrayed you! (*He collapses into a chair.*) I know it, I have no excuse (*he makes a sign to her not to speak*).

A great silence.

GERARD: (*his head in his hands*) That vision ... you and ... don't think that I'm interrogating you ... I know enough ... I know enough about it (*still a silence; he is absorbed in his thoughts, then*) The mystery is elsewhere.

FRANCES: I have only ever loved you, I swear it to you.

GERARD: Do you think I don't know that? (*Silence*)

FRANCES: Speak, crush me ... but not this silence. I know, I deserve everything (*she throws herself at his feet; he motions to her to rise and remains silent*). But why don't you speak? What is this horrible meditation?

GERARD: As it is, you didn't love him; your embrace was but the tussle of two bodies.

FRANCES: (*in tears*) I am not yet explaining myself ... it just happened.

GERARD: (*with a strange insistence*) Yes, it happened ... this filthy thing happened (*with an expressive gesture, as if to cut*), between us.

FRANCES: Do you think I am not ashamed? ... the most irreparable madness ...

GERARD: But this madness had its reasons.

FRANCES: I was bewildered, desperate ... you had rebuffed me ... The first requital that life offered me ...

GERARD: Don't try to explain ... your crime is not explained (in a low voice), but justifies itself. (*With a sort of pity infinitely distant.*) Get up (*he looks at her slowly as if in holy terror*). Marked, marked for every humiliation.

FRANCES: No! Not the insult of your forgiveness!

GERARD: I do not have to forgive you ... the reason for your actions is outside of you.

FRANCES: No, not that!. . .I would rather have death!

GERARD: There is no death for that which has never been. (*Falling to his knees.*) My God, we are not ... and you are.

FRANCES: I have lost him forever. (*A silence, one hears confusedly the prayer of Gerard; the words become more and more distinct.*)

GERARD: (*in prayer*) You have tempted me, then you've saved me. Here you have appeared like a sword of fire, and you have cut the knot that you yourself have formed. Everything has happened as you had wished ... from all eternity. My God, make my voice go to you like the prayer of a child. Once more I feel arise in me the sap of renewed souls.

FRANCES: (*with a gesture of supplication*) But me, Gerard, me! ...

GERARD: Here again I hear your voice which nothing may cover any more. Your voice is life, it is certainty.

FRANCES: (*striking her chest*) I who am suffering ...

GERARD: But I hear also, indistinct and painful, the cry of those who believe they are and who are no longer. I sense in the shadow their distraught gestures.

FRANCES: Will you have not a word, not a look of pity? Nothing but that senseless wisdom ... (*Gerard looks at her; the light which transfigures him goes out slowly; an expression of weariness, almost exhaustion appears on his face; he puts his hand on his chest.*) What's the matter? It looks like you are suffocating.

GERARD: (*feebly*) No, it's nothing.

FRANCES: Ah! I still prefer this discolored face and those lifeless eyes ... (*he has a strange smile on his face; she kisses him, he makes no resistance*).

GERARD: I am still not strong enough ... Ah! I need air! I'm suffocating!

FRANCES: (*stretching him on the sofa and undoing his collar*) Like that?

OLIVER: (*entering*) What's going on? Why is he like that?

FRANCES: He's dying, and I'm the one who has killed him.

OLIVER: Explain ...

FRANCES: You must do something ... the doctor ... I've lost my head ...

GERARD: (*in an indistinct voice*) No, there's nothing to be done ... it's getting better ... Oliver ... (*again a suffocation*).

FRANCES: We cannot stay like this ... I tell you that he lies here dying.

GERARD: (*making a sign to Oliver to approach*) Come ...

OLIVER: What is it? (*mimicry by Gerard, of accompanying words which one does not hear.*) (*In despai*r.) I don't understand you.

FRANCES: You must ... (*going to the door*). Martha!

GERARD: (*weakly*) Saved ... all roads have met together ...

OLIVER: Yes ...

GERARD: If you knew ...

FRANCES: (*at the door*) It's you ... listen (she goes out to speak to the maid).

GERARD: I must tell you ... and I cannot ... all that has happened ... the mysterious coming together of events ... the paths of Grace.

FRANCES: (*coming back*) Don't listen to him. He is delirious. None of that is true.

OLIVER: (*kneeling beside Gerard*) But it is real.

GERARD: (*casting an anxious look at him*) So then?

OLIVER: Yes, I deny that anything in the world can be more real than your belief ... it makes the world revolve around you. The strength of belief is surely the measure of being. (*Continually feeling Gerard's look weighing on him.*) That's not enough? Your faith is as real to my eyes as dreams and as life.

FRANCES: You are exhausting him.

GERARD: (*weakly*) No, no, more ...

OLIVER: It is more than truth, it is an act of creation; it is the living idea which creates and transforms ... some more? I still feel your anxiety weighing on me.

GERARD: (*indistinctly*) And Him?

OLIVER: He is the spirit that affirms his unity, he is the faith that transcends and projects ... still more? I cannot ... it is perhaps the supreme need of souls.

GERARD: (*raising himself painfully, with a cry*) God is free! (*He falls back heavily.*)

OLIVER: (*leaning over him*) Gerard! My friend!

FRANCES: (*desperately*) Ah! It's not possible! (*She throws herself over the inanimate body of Gerard. A silence during which one hears only her sobbing.*)

OLIVER: (*scrutinizing the mystery of the calm face*) Nothing more than a look ... And now, on the strength of that look ...

CURTAIN

(*March–April 1911*)

INTRODUCTION TO THE SANDCASTLE

Geoffrey Karabin

Existentialist philosophy is many things, but an embrace of the concrete is one of its most prominent elements. The concrete refers to real happenings in the life of the individual and his/her uniquely personal experience of reality. The fact that existentialist philosophers often turned to literature as well as theater to express their sense of life is a reflection of this embrace. It is in these forms that the dramas, victories, joys, and tragedies of life come to fruition in the most personal of terms.

Gabriel Marcel's work is located firmly within this effort to embrace the concrete dimensions of reality. In Marcel's philosophical writings, what begin as formal philosophical meditations invariably become reflections upon the experience of life. As an example, a meditation on theological dogma quickly becomes a question of whether religious belief is an opening to a shared experience of the divine or a mechanism to dominate others. Marcel extracts philosophical profundity from matters as mundane as why he believes Americans take a liking to hotel rooms and what a child giving some flowers to an adult says about the adult and the child. But more than anything else, Marcel's philosophy is a philosophy about relationships and how human beings open themselves to or close themselves off from others.

Given the intertwinement of the personal and the philosophical in Marcel's thought, it is not surprising that he takes his place amongst those existentialist philosophers who were also playwrights. The dramatic is not a side project to be dismissed in favor of his more purely philosophical works, but a flowering of his thought in a different form. For that reason, it is significant and an occasion of joy to have, for the first time, these two Marcelian plays translated into English. Not only Marcel scholars but all those who enjoy existentialist thought are given much to dwell upon in these dramatic works. Even more generally, those who enjoy reflecting upon the human condition, with its myriad challenges and ambiguities, have reason to thank Professor Traub for translating these plays for an English-speaking audience.

The Sandcastle: A Theater of Isolation

The Sandcastle is rich in philosophical themes that will occupy Marcel throughout his professional life. In this play, one discovers reflections on fidelity and death. One also finds Marcel dwelling upon questions of whether religious belief involves a denial or an embrace of life. There is a foray into the meaning of possession, amidst a host of other existentialist and Marcelian themes. While the play grapples with an array of topics, if one were looking for the central thought around which the action of The Sandcastle revolves, the concept of solitude emerges as a prime candidate.

Marcel once wrote that, "There is only one grief, to be alone."[24] One could read The Sandcastle as a meditation upon this insight. The two central figures of the work, Moirans and his daughter Clarisse, struggle with solitude. Moirans seeks salvation from solitude but the salvation he attains is fleeting. Clarisse, on the other hand, finds herself in communion with God only to have that communion disrupted and ultimately destroyed by the egotism of her father. The tension of the play revolves around the role that these two characters play in saving as well as condemning each other to solitude.

When considering the nature of solitude explored in The Sandcastle, the divergent trajectories of father and daughter are paramount. Moirans dwells in solitude only to briefly escape it. Nonetheless, the solitude in which he dwells does not correspond to social isolation. He is a public figure and one greatly esteemed by those who view him as a champion of the Catholic cause in France. Clarisse, on the other hand, enjoys a communion with the divine only to lose that communion and suffer an itinerant existence where she feels at home neither on earth nor with what lies beyond.

---

24 Gabriel Marcel in Etienne Gilson (ed.), *Le Coeur des autres in Existentalisme chrétien: Gabriel Marcel* (Paris: Plon, 1947), quoted in Jill Graper Hernandez, *Gabriel Marcel's Ethics of Hope: Evil, God and Virtue* (London: Bloomsbury, 2011), p. 90.

Yet, in contrast to her father, Clarisse's period of communion corresponds to a socially disengaged existence. She does not participate in social rituals common for her age nor is her life oriented around building relationships with others. She is viewed as an impenetrable and opaque soul. In sum, the man of the public is alone; whereas the isolated woman enjoys a profound form of companionship that is ultimately lost.

These thoughts pertain to a theme that Marcel will develop in other works. He remarks that physical presence is not the same as spiritual presence: "Proximity is in no way the source of fraternity."[25] To be by someone is not to be with someone. To be amongst others is not tantamount to sharing oneself with others nor to allowing others to penetrate the boundaries of one's life.

Moirans gives voice to this philosophical dichotomy of presence/absence when he confesses that, "I wish you had pity on me, Peter. I am very much alone, I am horribly alone. All those people who were here earlier—you haven't seen them—they are so distant, and one must talk to them as if they were very close. One cannot depict, you see, what that solitude can be." (Act One, Scene Thirteen). It is at this moment—the moment that Moirans confesses his alienation from his purported friends, colleagues, and allies—that he invokes his hope for salvation: "Peter: Are you really so alone? Your youngest daughter ... Moirans: Clarisse? What do you know? I've hoped, yes ... without her, without the joy of seeing her grow and shine, I would have become ... I don't know ... a poor rag, a wreck of intelligence. But she is so secret, so closed." (Act One, Scene Thirteen.) Moirans' hope does not lie in his friends or colleagues, nor in his wife, to whom he reveals his complete spiritual separation in a particularly sad and dispiriting moment of the play. His hope lies in Clarisse. Moirans views his daughter as the antidote to his spiritual isolation. He senses in Clarisse a kindred soul. In her spiritual journey, he senses his own self being recreated.

The Curse of Egotism

Unfortunately, Moirans' sense of spiritual companionship is tainted with egotism. Egotism, along with its antipode of intersubjectivity, constitute

25 *Gabriel Marcel, Thou Shall Not Die*, ed. Anne Marcel and trans. Katharine Rose Hanley (South Bend, IN: St. Augustine's Press, 2009), p. 17.

central pillars of Marcel's philosophical interests. His exploration of egotism finds a dramatic outlet in the figure of Moirans. Moirans not only views his daughter as the mechanism to his salvation, but he is willing to sabotage Clarisse's deepest spiritual yearning so as to obtain this salvation. The sabotage is realized when Moirans resorts to a form of spiritual blackmail in the effort to prevent Clarisse from entering the convent. Moirans proclaims to Clarisse that, "If you inflict on me the deadly pain of seeing you bury yourself in the oblivion of the cloister, there will only be salvation for me in action .... I will only be able to give up this existence that has become necessary to me if you stay; we will leave together, we will travel...." (Act Three, Scene Five.) Clarisse is forced to choose between her yearning for the religious life and what she views as her father's spiritual suicide. For Clarisse, entering the convent would involve the forfeiture of her father's hoped-for conversion and salvation.

Yet because Clarisse hopes for her father's salvation via his re-unification with the divine, her renunciation of the convent only carries a short-term respite for Moirans' spiritual anguish. What the father receives in Clarisse's renunciation is not a companion who embraces his spiritual pride nor one who forsakes religious belief. He does not receive a spiritual counterpart to his own self, but a soul that is heartbroken by the loss of religious life. For it is not to be with him, but to act for him, that Clarisse offers her sacrifice.

The realization of this difference as well as the monstrosity of Moirans' egotism constitutes the culminating moment of the play. Clarisse chooses companionship with her mother over a partnership with her father. The dialogue is tragic: "Moirans (crying out): My little one ... you are all that I have left. Clarisse: And for her? What is left for her? Moirans (with contempt): Her!" (Act Four, Scene Eleven.) Moirans not only loses his salvation, but he loses his possession, his prized daughter, to what he regards as the inferior cause of his wife's well-being.

In seeking to save himself from isolation, Moirans in fact guarantees it by failing to allow others their own reality, or to recognize their value independent of his use for them. Because he has no use for those he considers beneath him, including his wife, eldest daughter, and son, Moirans abandons the hope of a relationship with them. Yet his remaining hope—the hope of a relationship with and salvation through Clarisse—is made impossible because of his denial of her spiritual reality.

Authenticity versus Inauthenticity

Solitude is portrayed as the outgrowth of egotism. Solitude is also the gateway to another major theme of the work. The divorce between Moirans' public persona and his private solitude raises the question of who he really is. In the terms of existential philosophy, the issue is one of authenticity versus inauthenticity. Is the authentic Moirans the public champion of Christianity or the figure ensconced in the private image of himself as a man beyond the need of religious belief? The question is fascinating, at least in part, because Moirans himself seems incapable of a definitive answer. The issue is not one of simplistic duplicity on Moirans' part. One of the play's central struggles is whether Moirans adopts the view of the Bishop, who locates the essence of Moirans' soul in his Catholic identity, or whether Moirans understands himself, as his daughter Clarisse urges, to be an unbeliever. This struggle represents not merely the pull of two powerful forces in Moirans' life, but the effort of the official Church to claim spiritual ownership of one of its members.

The Bishop insists on a private audience with Moirans after hearing that Moirans is considering renouncing his official post and thereby abandoning his position as a public champion of Christianity. Moirans affirms the truth of the rumors and confesses the absence of religious belief in his soul. At this juncture, the Bishop challenges Moirans and declares that Moirans will not send his letter of resignation. Moirans responds: "My lord, you don't see that I am no longer capable, that it would only be a masquerade. I am no longer Catholic." (Act Four, Scene Eleven.) The Bishop, anticipating this response, offers his thesis:

> For ten minutes I've been expecting that sentence. Do you think one can stop being a Catholic? One does not cease being a Catholic just as one never ceases being a creature. You think that Catholicism is like a color with which our thinking is tinted, and which can be erased by the influence of I don't know what reflections and I don't know what experiences (*extending his hand*), I do not wish to know them. But no. He is in us well beyond what we can attain, well beyond what we can change: what we can attain and change is so little! Cease to be Catholic! You

remind me—pardon this anecdote—of a small child, who seeing himself maltreated by his classmates and noticing that they never hit his sister, said: "Papa, I don't want to be a little boy anymore." Your religion is in you, but it is not of you (Act Four, Scene Eleven).

The Bishop's challenge is not that Moirans ought to retain the post for the sake of appearances. He challenges Moirans to recognize his current state as a passing crisis that masks the truth of his religious identity. Moirans' true self, as the Bishop remarks at another juncture, "is that of a son of the Church" (Act Four, Scene Eleven). The Bishop asserts that Moirans' authentic self is discovered in God's will, not in the self-generated image of the apostate.

Clarisse does not adopt the Bishop's view. Where the Bishop finds the workings of divine providence, Clarisse discovers a spiritual betrayal. Her burgeoning awareness of this betrayal begins with her disgust at her father's treatment of his eldest daughter, Theresa. Faced with the scandal of his daughter's divorce, Moirans withholds his consent for the divorce:

Clarisse: My God, what I was afraid of is true; it's because of people's opinions that you oppose Theresa's divorce!
Moirans: Childishness again. Do I busy myself about what people will say in general?
Clarisse: It is not the thought of Theresa's salvation ...
Moirans: Theresa's salvation! If I object to her divorce, it is forbidden that my daughter's actions contradict me. It is about me, do you clearly understand the difference?
Clarisse: I don't want to understand. In my eyes this amounts to the same thing (Act One, Scene Fourteen).

Clarisse's fear is that her father's faith is adopted for public consumption or perhaps for the sake of a self-image that he wishes to maintain rather than a genuine expression of religious devotion. This fear is fully realized with his spiritual blackmail, where Moirans shows himself willing to sacrifice Clarisse's spiritual salvation for his hoped-for escape from solitude.

While the blackmail serves as the culmination of his spiritual inauthenticity, Clarisse's growing conviction that Moirans serves not God but his own self receives support in other moments of the play. Perhaps most damning to Clarisse is her realization that Moirans is unable to relate to the spiritual call that generates her desire to enter the convent. Moirans responds to the revelation of Clarisse's vocation by mapping it onto the elementary stages of his own spiritual journey. In Moirans' view, the religious call constitutes a passing fancy. Despite abandoning the call later in the play, Clarisse never renounces the truth of its source nor the conviction that one is meant to serve the divine. It is this realization that ultimately denies the potential for true communion between father and daughter.

That Clarisse abandons her religious vocation without renouncing the sincerity of the call inspires a final thought with regard to the concepts of authenticity and inauthenticity. As it turns out, the question of authenticity is not only for Moirans to grapple with; it is one which Clarisse must confront as well. Moirans plants seeds of doubt in Clarisse's soul by claiming that she may be pursuing the convent for the sake of spiritual comfort and ease. She comes to question whether her desire to enter the convent is really a desire to escape the trials of life and the spiritual tribulations attendant upon one who doesn't rest on the faux certainties offered to those of the cloistered life. She is forced to confront the possibility that her desire to enter the convent is an effort to assure herself temporal tranquility on the way to eternal bliss. In an impassioned dialogue with the family priest, Clarisse makes it clear that it is not the sacrifice of physical pleasures or worldly delights that trouble her. What troubles her is that in entering the convent she may be taking the spiritually easy way out. "Clarisse: If little by little one forgets that the gate of heaven is a narrow gate, if one's mind is dulled by easy certainties and ... (*With fright*) ... I no longer know, I no longer know" (Act Three, Scene Seven). She comes to see the convent as a temptation to exchange spiritual growth for the complacency of the cloistered life.

While the question of authenticity arises for both Moirans and Clarisse, it is important to note a fundamental difference between the two. Clarisse's crisis revolves around the question of whether she is remaining true to her religious calling. Moirans' crisis revolves around whether he ever genuinely believed. Clarisse's crisis came in the service to a higher truth; Moirans' is centered on whether he was serving only himself or surreptitiously doing the work of God. Perhaps Marcel confirms Clarisse's other-oriented and faith-based disposition as well as providing a clue to Moirans' true nature, when the play closes with Moirans' utter solitude in comparison to Clarisse finding herself called to offer companionship to her mother. This is only a hint, however, from Marcel. Life asks the questions; the individual is called upon to make the right judgment.

THE SANDCASTLE
(Le Palais de sable)
A PLAY IN FOUR ACTS

TRANSLATED FROM THE FRENCH BY MARIA TRAUB

CAST OF CHARACTERS

Moirans, 52 years old.

Peter Servant, 32 years old.

Father Grandin, 64 years old.

Bishop Vielle, 60 years old.

De Mézidon, 55 years old.

Henry Moirans, 26 years old.

De Lucé, 60 years old.

De Durnat, 55 years old.

Drouet, 48 years old.

Clarisse Moirans, 21 years old.

Mrs. Moirans, 50 years old.

Theresa Needier, 25 years old.

Mrs. De Lucé, 50 years old.

Miss De Rives, 26 years old.

Miss De Terny, 35 years old.

The first three acts in a small town about 50 kilometers from Paris; the fourth by the shore of an Italian lake.

ACT ONE

A large room, welcoming and formal, in a beautiful old country house in the provinces. In the background, two tall French doors open onto a terrace.

Act One: Scene One

Moirans, Mrs. Moirans, Miss De Rives, Henry, Mr. De Lucé, Mrs. De Lucé, De Durnat, Miss De Terny, Drouet, etc....

MRS. DE LUCÉ: (*to Moirans*) You have been admirable, and the Ministry will not recover from it.

MISS DE TERNY: Have you read the article in *The Paris News*? It's rightly said, that speech is the death-knell of a regime.

MRS. DE LUCÉ: The despicable regime.

MISS DE TERNY: Finally! It's just that we were beginning to despair.

MISS DE RIVES: Do you know what I'm learning? There are copies set aside and he did not say so (*to Moirans*). You're are a measly one.

MOIRANS: (*laughing*) Come on, Henry, find them.

DE LUCÉ: This discourse should be spread; it should be posted in the center of the town.

MRS. DE LUCÉ: (*to Mrs. Moirans*) My husband is in a state of exultation! I have not seen him like this since the great days.

DE LUCÉ: Since Rennes.

MRS. DE LUCÉ: He woke me up at night to read some lines.

MOIRANS: (*to De Durnat*) Even so, you are exaggerating a little bit, I assure you.

DE DURNAT: No, no, everyone has said: a Christian Mirabeau.[26]

MISS DE TERNY: The most beautiful gift to the service of the most beautiful cause.

DROUET: (*smiling, to Moirans*) There is one whom we will not need to ask if she has read *The Paris News*[27] —she is quoting it.

MISS DE RIVES: Well? These extra copies?

MRS. MOIRANS: We are looking for them, my dear child. (*To De Durnat*) You were there?

DE DURNAT: If I was there!

MRS. MOIRANS: Just imagine that at the last moment, he no longer wished to speak. He said: what good is it?

MISS DE TERNY: What good is it!

DE DURNAT: And it is you, dear lady, you who have rekindled his courage. You have done beautiful work, and all the mothers of France will be grateful to you. We will no longer hear talk about the monopoly of education in fifty years.

---

26 Honoré Gabriel Riqueti, Count of Mirabeau (9 March 1749 – 2 April 1791) was a leader of the early stages of the French Revolution. A noble, he was involved in numerous scandals before the start of the Revolution in 1789 that had left his reputation in ruins.

27 *L'Écho de Paris* was a daily newspaper in Paris from 1884 to 1944. The paper's editorial stance was initially conservative and nationalistic.

MISS DE TERNY: He has cast out the ghost. And the public school ...

DE LUCÉ: The infamous school ...

MRS. DE LUCÉ: It will not recover from the blows you have given it.

MOIRANS: *(to Rouet)* It's what they believe, as they say!

MISS DE TERNY: *(to Mrs. Moirans)* He does not seem content enough: the savior of France should have a different face.

MRS. MOIRANS: It's that he is tired. He's a nervous one, you know. He tenses up, his body tightens as a result of his effort. And then afterwards, nothing.

DE DURNAT: We have felt the flame rise in him, little by little.

MISS DE TERNY: *(looking at the article)* Oh! This conclusion!

MISS DE RIVES *(to Henry who is bringing some brochures)*: Here are some additional copies. Distribute them *(She pages them feverishly)*. Oh! They have skipped some of it.

MOIRANS: *(smiling)* Well no, my dear young lady, I promise you, they have skipped nothing!

MISS DE RIVES: Ah! There it is ... Oh! This passage! "Gentlemen, at this hour where everywhere clouds are gathering over our heads, where even the blindest, the most willfully blind, tremble before the terrible visions of to-morrow, there will be a voice to tell you that the most formidable danger is not where you think. Gentlemen, the most formidable danger is not at the border, it is in you. You are bad surgeons, gentlemen, you do not know how to put the blade in the right place. You will in vain increase the numbers, build barracks, and pile up the texts of the laws, and sow millions by the fist-fuls: all that is essential, but it is all in vain. It is in vain that soldiers will run to the ramparts to protect the city that God no longer protects. You laugh, gentlemen, and this laughter is irreligious. Those valiant ones who will give their blood tomorrow—because they will give it, I affirm—what promises will sustain them at the frightful moment of agony? During those decisive years when one forms a character and a belief, you have taught them that everything ends on this earth, that there is no consoling angel to carry to God like a holy wreath, the souls of those who have died. Patiently, for a long time, and with a deceitful concern—in the name of what mediocre and nebulous philosophies—you have uprooted in them the hopes that help people live … and die. I ask you, gentlemen, what image will rise up before those dying? They will not see in a light of honorable exaltation, a saved and grateful country extend toward them its maternal arms—for the country, the country you've told them, is only a relative notion. A relative notion! What! Is it for a relative notion that they must spill their blood? Gentlemen, the irony is cruel … and you wonder that some are hesitant and rebel? A relative notion! Gentlemen, they will march, I believe it, I am sure of it, but if at the tragic moment some of them yield—I cannot endure this terrible thought— I am suggesting that those truly responsible would be you!"

Act One: Scene Two

The same characters; Father Grandin

FATHER GRANDIN: Continue, continue! I only wish to present my congratulations to our distinguished orator for his wonderful speech.

MRS. MOIRANS: Reverend Father, in spite of your rheumatism … but what lack of attention to yourself, really!

FATHER GRANDIN: Madam, there are no rheumatisms that can resist the emotion which possesses me at this moment. And I must even repeat to you the appreciation that my lord Bishop …

MRS. MOIRANS: What! My lord Bishop …

FATHER GRANDIN: That my lord Bishop has kindly wished to weigh in on this remarkable piece of eloquence; he has formulated his thought in these terms, which each one of us can admire, as I do, for their appropriateness and sobriety: "They are, he said, the words of a Christian and those of a Frenchman." In expressing himself like that, I think I can say that my lord Bishop was the interpreter, especially authorized, by the way, of this general feeling which makes me also exclaim: Mr. Deputy, you have deserved from the Church and from the nation; on behalf of the Church and of the nation, thanks ... (*general emotion; everyone speaks at the same time*).

MOIRANS: Reverend Father, believe that I am profoundly touched by the words that you have just addressed to me in your name and that of my lord Bishop ... I ... (*he is searching for his words*).

FATHER GRANDIN: I see you now at this moment just as I knew you more than forty years ago, Mr. Deputy ... (to the others). Yes, our acquaintance does not date to yesterday ... I see you again as a curly-headed and mischievous toddler ... You were very mischievous, Mr. Deputy, and I used to scold you sometimes against my will ... and before this vision, a great emotion, a very sweet emotion came over me ... My son, embrace me. (*General emotion.*)

MISS DE TERNY: If all those atheists were witness to this scene ...

MOIRANS: Reverend Father, would it be too much of an imposition to ask you to spend a moment with our old housekeeper, who is ill, as you know, and to whom your visit would bring great pleasure?

FATHER GRANDIN: But of course. Very willingly; (*to Henry*) my son, take me to her. (*He goes out with Henry.*)

Act One: Scene Three

The same characters, minus Reverend Father and Henry

MRS. DE LUCÉ: (*to Mr. Moirans*) Miss Amelia is still the same? (*Miss Amelia is an elderly housekeeper, ailing and bedridden.*)

Mrs. De MOIRANS: She is doing a little better; she is very well cared for.

MRS. DE LUCÉ: By that young doctor? Don't rely too much upon him. There are some disagreeable rumors going around town about him.

MISS DE TERNY: Yes, I do not think he is a very good Catholic.

MRS. MOIRANS: My husband has really struck up a friendship with him; he says that he is very intelligent.

Mr. MOIRANS: I only mean that at least we have a doctor.

MISS DE TERNY: Really, should you speak like that? And Dr. Morillot?

MOIRANS: Between us, let's agree that he is an ignoramus.

MRS. DE LUCÉ: He's an old-fashioned doctor.

DE LUCÉ: But what is it that makes you say that he is no longer the best?

MRS. DE LUCÉ: He doesn't give in to all this nonsense ...

DE LUCÉ: But what says that he's wrong?

MRS. DE LUCÉ: You will not deny that he is a perfectly honest man.

MISS DE TERNY: I meet him every Sunday at Saint Francis.

MRS. DE LUCÉ: We cannot say that about Dr. Servan.

MOIRANS: He's a very distinguished boy and after all, his religious opinions do not concern us.

MISS DE TERNY: But think of all the dedication and self-sacrifice that a doctor must exert; how can he do it if he believes in nothing? As for myself, it would be impossible for me to trust in ...

MRS. DE LUCÉ: It's clear. (*to Mrs. Moirans*) And Clarisse, that dear child, won't we see her?

MRS. MOIRANS: She's been a little tired for a few days; she herself insisted on staying by the bedside of Miss Amelia.

MISS DE TERNY: Dear little one! And her clinic still occupies her so much?

MRS. MOIRANS: Always. Her life is divided between the clinic and the church.

MISS DE TERNY: A holy life.

MRS. DE LUCÉ: A holy life but an austere one for so young a girl. She allows herself no distraction?

MRS. MOIRANS: Clarisse has a horror of the world.

MRS. DE LUCÉ: All the same, you should get her to go out a little. It is not natural at her age not to like balls.

MRS. MOIRANS: Do you think I haven't tried very often? But she is like her father: what he says or nothing, it's the same thing. (*She chuckles.*)

Act One: Scene Four

The same characters; Clarisse

MRS. DE LUCÉ: Here is the angel. We were just speaking about you; and I was saying to your mama that it wasn't reasonable on your part, at your age and with your beauty (*Clarisse has a nervous movement*), to cloister yourself like this. You will ruin your health, my dear, I am telling you. The balls, the evening parties …

CLARISSE: But if all that bores me, madam, what can I do?

MRS. DE LUCÉ: You don't know what it is. There doesn't exist a girl who doesn't like going to a dance.

MRS. MOIRANS: My daughter is an original; she refused to go hear the speech of her father.

MISS DE RIVES: No, is it true?

CLARISSE: That would have made me uncomfortable.

MRS. MOIRANS: It's true that Clarisse cannot stand crowds. One day she fainted (*a silence*).

CLARISSE: Mama, did Theresa come back?

MISS DE TERNY: Your older daughter is here?

MRS. MOIRANS: (*embarrassed*) She came to spend a few days with us.

MRS. DE LUCÉ: She is doing well?

MRS. MOIRANS: I thank you.

MRS. DE LUCÉ: Her husband is a charming man. I remember having chatted an entire evening with him. His conversation is genuine fireworks.

DE DURNAT: (*to Moirans, who has heard and who has smiled*): Admit, my dear Deputy, that the current situation cannot continue.

MOIRANS: Don't you notice that there have been men in every age to say this of every situation?

DE DURNAT: You will not deny that we are in an epoch of transition, even crisis.

DE LUCÉ: It's obvious.

MOIRANS: In every epoch the opposition has believed itself to be in a time of crisis.

DE DURNAT: All things considered, we're going to ruin, at 100 kilometers an hour.

MOIRANS: The ruin of what?

DE LUCÉ and DE DURNAT: (*together*) Of France!

DE DURNAT: My dear Deputy, you are in a paradoxical mood today; admit it. This country is decomposing and in a few years from now it will only be a prey for a foreign invasion, didn't you say so yourself?

DE LUCÉ: It is very obvious.

MOIRANS: So be it. You are right.

DE DURNAT: When we will only be a German province ...

MISS DE TERNY: How awful!

DE DURNAT: You have to face the facts.

DE LUCÉ: There will not be found a Frenchman to endure such shame.

DROUET: You think so?

DE LUCÉ: I am sure, sir; I have been an officer.

MOIRANS: In all events it is an ending for the distant future; beforehand, we'll see many others.

MRS. DE LUCÉ: (*to Mrs. Moirans*) Myself, I admit that I would only have confidence in an overthrow of the government.

MISS DE TERNY: Or in a miracle perhaps.

DROUET: There is no miracle in a democracy, miss.

MOIRANS: (*to Drouet*) It's profound, what you just said.

MISS DE TERNY: (*to Mrs. Moirans*) Have you read in the *Gazette*[28] what happened at Our Lady of Roncière?

MRS. MOIRANS: I was very impressed.

MRS. DE LUCÉ: I am thinking of making a pilgrimage there this autumn.

MISS DE TERNY: What a good idea!

MRS. DE LUCÉ: What holds me back a little, I admit it, is that it must smell really bad.

MRS. MOIRANS: Did you note the allusions made by Reverend Father Jorette the other Sunday?

MISS DE TERNY: He's a marvelous preacher, we have nothing to envy in Paris.

MRS. MOIRANS: He noted some coincidences that really struck me.

MISS DE TERNY: In Italy, the disaster of Messina, right? If these wretches remain in power we can expect some scary things.

MRS. DE LUCÉ: Who knows if the flooding ... (*a frightened silence, Clarisse rises*).

MRS. MOIRANS: You are leaving already?

28 *La Gazette*, originally *Gazette de France*, was the first weekly magazine published in France. It was founded by Théophraste Renaudot and published its first edition on 30 May 1631. It progressively became the mouthpiece of one royalist faction, the Legitimists. *La Gazette* disappeared in 1915.

CLARISSE: I'm going to see if Miss Amelia needs anything.

MRS. MOIRANS: The Reverend Father is with her. (*Clarisse sits down, nervously.*)

DE DURNAT: The elections portend quite badly. These scoundrels will not give us their votes this time (*to Moirans*). You, naturally, you have nothing to fear, with your personal situation. You will not even need to campaign.

MOIRANS: You think so? You think that I don't have to offer political campaigns to my constituents? Well! I can tell you that you are far from the truth. In this disgusting profession, no one is exempt. When I think of the abject nature of the opposition, it seems that I will no longer be able … and that I would do better to plant my cabbages.[29]

DE DURNAT: Don't say that; we have need of you. It's one more sacrifice that you are making for the cause.

MOIRANS: All that is so vain … so vain. One good will against this rising tide … (*he remains pensive a moment, eyes fixed*).

Act One: Scene Five

The same characters; Reverend Father Grandin

FATHER GRANDIN: I've just spent some edifying minutes by the side of that holy person.

CLARISSE: (*rising*) I'm going to her side for a little while; she doesn't like to remain alone. (*She goes out.*)

FATHER GRANDIN: (*to Mrs. Moirans, while the others are chatting*) I've had the pleasant surprise of just now meeting Mrs. Naudier; I didn't know that she was here.

---

29 Allusion to the idea of "cultivating one's garden," found in Voltaire's *Candide*.

MRS. MOIRANS: Theresa arrived last night; this is a big concern for us, Reverend Father.

FATHER GRANDIN: The rumors that have reached me, do they have some basis? Is this poor young woman ...

MRS. MOIRANS: It is only too true.

FATHER GRANDIN: I hope that she bears as a Christian the trials that Providence ...

MRS. MOIRANS: Alas! Reverend Father ...

FATHER GRANDIN: The moment is hardly favorable for such a discussion.

MRS. MOIRANS: I will have great need of your counsel, Reverend Father.

FATHER GRANDIN: My modest experience is entirely at your service.

MRS. DE LUCÉ: (*rising, to her husband*) Gaston, it's late, we would do well to think about leaving (*all rise*).

MISS DE TERNY: (*to Mrs. Moirans*) Try to get Clarisse to come to see us; we will be so pleased ...

MRS. MOIRANS: She is so singular!

FATHER GRANDIN: She seemed anxious just now; this dear child, would she have some concern?

MRS. MOIRANS: Not that I know of, Reverend Father.

MOIRANS: (*with uneasiness*) Really, Reverend father, you noticed ...

FATHER GRANDIN: I may be wrong.

MISS DE RIVES: No, no, Reverend Father is surely right.

MRS. DE LUCÉ: (*to Mrs. Moirans*) Don't torment yourself; at that age you become melancholy over very little.

MRS. MOIRANS: Clarisse is so tight-lipped.

FATHER GRANDIN: I was about to forget an important errand; Mr. De Mézidon asked me to tell you that he would be coming to see you shortly.

MOIRANS: (*rather dryly*) I fear I know why he is coming.

MRS. MOIRANS: (*at half-voice*) How boring! Will it be necessary to have him stay for dinner? (*Separate goodbyes and handshakes; Mrs. Moirans to Mrs. De Lucé, while showing her out.*) Kiss your Yvonne fondly for me; Henry would have liked so much for you to bring her!

FATHER GRANDIN: (*to Moirans*) Don't be too hard on that poor Mr. De Mézidon.

Act One: Scene Six

Moirans, Mrs. Moirans

MRS. MOIRANS: The story about Theresa has already made the rounds in town; Reverend Father was aware of it.

MOIRANS: Clarisse, why was she concerned?

MRS. MOIRANS: I don't know how to win over the obstinacy of Theresa.

MOIRANS: Clarisse knows nothing about this story? You haven't told her anything about it?

MRS. MOIRANS: I did not say a word about it; it must have been Theresa herself.

MOIRANS: (*sharply*) I have forbidden her to do it.

MRS. MOIRANS: You cannot prevent Theresa from confiding in her sister.

MOIRANS: There is no longer any real intimacy between them, since Theresa's marriage.

MRS. MOIRANS: What do you know?

MOIRANS: I've noticed it.

MRS. MOIRANS: (*bitterly*) Clarisse has shared secrets with you?

MOIRANS: That wasn't necessary.

MRS. MOIRANS: You have the pretentiousness to read into her heart?

MOIRANS: I know that she keeps no secrets from me.

MRS. MOIRANS: And yet you cannot explain her behavior just now.

MOIRANS: She will tell me what it's about, if I ask her.

MRS. MOIRANS: But will you ask her?

MOIRANS: I don't know.

MRS. MOIRANS: You will do well to abstain; if you encounter a refusal it would be too mortifying for you. (*A heavy silence.*) And about Theresa's situation ... I am sure that she is still at Professor Pigault's.

MOIRANS: If that amuses her.

MRS. MOIRANS: You're not taking her decision seriously?

MOIRANS: Not for a minute. In defying me, she knows to what she is exposing herself.

MRS. MOIRANS: You are terrible, Roger … Here she is.

Act One: Scene Seven

The same characters; Theresa

MOIRANS: Did you tell your sister what I told you—to keep quiet?

THERESA: I have not yet been able to chat with her; tonight she will know everything.

MOIRANS : So you have the firm intention of defying me?

THERESA: Why shouldn't she know of my unhappiness?

MOIRANS: (*with disdain*) Your unhappiness! … You are not answering my question.

THERESA: I'm waiting for someone to explain this sanction.

MOIRANS: I do not have to justify my orders.

THERESA: (*to her mother*) What a tyrant!

MOIRANS: You do not impress me. If Clarisse is made aware of this filth, I am telling you that you will not remain here.

THERESA: You are too afraid of scandal … I am not afraid of you.

MRS. MOIRANS: But listen to me for a moment, Roger; the little one will learn sooner or later ...

MOIRANS: No matter; I know how sensitive she is; she reacts in a profound, mysterious way. The story of her sister could shake her decisively, disgust her with marriage, what do I know?

THERESA: You want her ignorant then? She must come to marriage like a little child?

MOIRANS: I fear nothing for her. The man that she will marry ...

THERESA: You know him!

MOIRANS: (*continuing*)...Whoever it is will not resemble the one you are complaining about. Besides, didn't we warn you? You are the one who wanted to marry him.

THERESA: I acknowledge it, I was mistaken ... I have paid for it quite dearly, my fault. (*She is crying*).

MOIRANS: These tears will not soften me.

MRS. MOIRANS: Roger!

MOIRANS: A fault like yours is not paid for, it is expiated.

MRS. MOIRANS: You are harsh.

THERESA: Then through all my life I will have to drag myself after this wretch because ...

MOIRANS: You have permission to separate from him.

THERESA: And then what? Vegetate like an old maid who is no longer innocent, who knows what love can be!

MOIRANS: Your regrets disgust me.

THERESA: All this so as not to disturb the beautiful arrangement of your life, so that it is not said: "You know the famous Catholic? He has a daughter who is divorced." It is egotism, it's monstrous.

MRS. MOIRANS: Theresa, you know very well, that religion ...

THERESA: It's not my religion.

MOIRANS: It is ours.

THERESA: It's not a religion, it's a prison.

MOIRANS: It's a safeguard, the only one against wickedness.

THERESA: I will divorce.

MOIRANS: So be it, but you will not see us again.

THERESA: One more deliverance.

MRS. MOIRANS: Theresa! Can you speak like this?

THERESA: I have had enough! For a long time you've treated me like the unsuccessful one; everything was for her ...

MRS. MOIRANS: Theresa, have I neglected you?

THERESA: You, that doesn't ... (*she stops*). But him, has he tried to conceal his favoritism? Especially since my operation ... and that ... that I cannot forgive him.

MRS. MOIRANS: Theresa, you know very well that is not true.

THERESA: No, it's not false. I remember the look with which he received me when I came down for the first time; a look so disdainful, so cruel!

MRS. MOIRANS: Theresa, you know nevertheless how unhappy we all have been.

THERESA: A woman who will never have children, for him I no longer counted.

MRS. MOIRANS: Roger, say that it's not true.

MOIRANS: I do not have to justify myself ... These are old stories over which there is no going back. One thing is certain: between what Theresa calls life, love (*with a shiver of disgust*), love and us, she will have to choose. (*He goes out.*)

Act One: Scene Eight

Mrs. Moirans; Theresa

MRS. MOIRANS: My poor daughter, I pity you with all my heart.

THERESA: I don't want people to pity me. My decision is made. You will not see me again.

MRS. MOIRANS: Theresa, before deciding anything, promise me one thing.

THERESA: What, mama?

MRS. MOIRANS: One little thing. I have not been a very demanding mother, admit it.

THERESA: (*with a pale smile*) It's true.

MRS. MOIRANS: You're smiling ... Don't you know that it's I who have been the unhappiest one here?

THERESA: Don't say that mama. There are things in life that I know that you are not aware of. Father can be a mean man, he's not a ... (*she stops*).

MRS. MOIRANS: There is nothing worse than what has been my life: to be treated like a thing, like a zero ...

THERESA: After what I have known, it's still happiness. (*A silence.*)

MRS. MOIRANS: My little one ... let me send you Reverend Father Grandin. I'm sure that he will convince you. Life hasn't changed to that point. I remember when you were small, in catechism class, you were always among those who answered the best.

THERESA: My poor mama, what do you want me to say to you?

MRS. MOIRANS: For others of us ... suffering used to give us more faith, more religion ... and you ... one could say it's the opposite.

THERESA: Mama, I know nothing about the other life, I don't want to know anything about it. I know that I'm an unhappy woman.

MRS. MOIRANS: My little one ... Providence must know what it is doing.

THERESA: Providence ... (*she has a kind of hysterical laughter*). Well! Providence has not suffered as I have, and it sticks its nose in funny things ... Providence ... No, you see I cannot believe that. And then why sacrifice my life. Without knowing why; renouncing so many things ... what difference does it make to God? ... if he exists ... I don't know, someone can still love me ... I'm not old yet ... a good man ... I'm not asking for him to be very intelligent.

MRS. MOIRANS: You're right, go on; men who are too intelligent ...

THERESA: You cannot know, mama; at just the idea that a man would still be able to tell me things ... some tender things ... I ... (*she bursts into sobs*).

Act One: Scene Nine

The same characters; Clarisse

CLARISSE: What's happening? Why is Theresa crying?

MRS. MOIRANS: It's nothing ... a little nervousness.

CLARISSE: Mama, you mustn't hide anything from me; I want to know why Theresa is crying.

MRS. MOIRANS: Your father ...

CLARISSE: It's like his letters ... you didn't let me read them. Why? I cannot live in this atmosphere ... Lies (*she brings her hand to her chest*) ... I feel stifled.

MRS. MOIRANS: I assure you dear one, don't question us.

CLARISSE: Why? I've never seen Theresa like this (*to her sister*). You, Theresa, answer me. (*Theresa makes a sign that she cannot.*) What have I done so that no one has confidence in me anymore? (*She wrings her hands.*)

MRS. MOIRANS: Your father has forbidden us ...

CLARISSE: Him, forbidden?

Act One: Scene Ten

The same characters; Moirans

CLARISSE: Father, is it true that you have forbidden people to tell me the truth?

MOIRANS: My dear one ... it's for your own good.

CLARISSE: It's not possible. I am no longer a child. What is my good, no one can know but me, not even you.

MOIRANS: Clarisse ... you are still so young ...

CLARISSE: Those are mama's phrases; you shouldn't ...

MOIRANS: And I used to believe that you had confidence in me. At the first trial that confidence comes up short.

CLARISSE: That confidence, you are abusing it by asking me for it. (*A silence.*)

MOIRANS: Listen ...

CLARISSE: Father, tell me the truth ... (*with remorse*) pardon!

MOIRANS: Your sister has consulted a doctor. You know that operation that she had last year ...

.

CLARISSE: Well?

MOIRANS: It has left traces such ... that Theresa will never have children.

CLARISSE: Never have children!

MOIRANS: Never. Do you understand now?

CLARISSE: Theresa! (*She embraces her.*) My poor Theresa! How I pity you! (*A silence; she is crying*) ... Never any children ... it's awful ... we used to talk about them so often before ... so I'll never be Aunt Clarisse ... the children of Henry, it will not be the same (*she breaks into sobs*).

MOIRANS: (*uneasily*) Aunt Clarisse? What do you mean?

CLARISSE: My poor, poor Theresa! But why hide it from me?

MOIRANS: I was seeing you so tired, so unwell ...

CLARISSE: I had the right to share such pain. And it's only recently? Why was it not seen immediately?

MOIRANS: I cannot explain it to you ... they are questions that are too technical.

CLARISSE: And your husband Theresa ... (*to her parents*). Let me speak alone with her, I implore you.

MOIRANS: (*to Theresa, on the side*): You remember!

MRS. MOIRANS: (*in a low voice to Theresa*) My darling, I'm begging you ... for me ... do it for me.

THERESA: I will see. (*She goes out with Clarisse.*)

Act One: Scene Eleven

Moirans, Mrs. Moirans; then Peter

MRS. MOIRANS: Roger, you shouldn't have ... sooner or later she will know that there is something else; she will not forgive you for having deceived her.

MOIRANS: Me she will forgive ... (*with anguish*). But what did she want to say?

PETER: (*entering, to Mrs. Moirans*) Hello, madam.

MOIRANS: I believe you will be satisfied with your patient, doctor. Last night was very good; she is getting back an appetite.

PETER: She has a very solid constitution. Without it she could not have held up.

MRS. MOIRANS: (*to Peter*) Will you follow me doctor? (*She goes out with him.*)

Act One: Scene Twelve

Moirans remains alone, preoccupied. A maid announces:
Mr. De Mézidon.

MOIRANS: Show him in.

DE MÉZIDON: Hello, my dear Deputy. I hope that the Reverend Father didn't forget to announce me?

MOIRANS: No, no, I was expecting you.

DE MÉZIDON: I wanted first to congratulate you on your remarkable speech, and then also ...

MOIRANS: Spare yourself the circumlocutions, dear sir; I think I've guessed what you have come to ask me.

DE MÉZIDON: No more to say: you are an excellent man. Well, yes, my dear Deputy, I come to ask you to intervene in the Chamber on a point which for me, for us, touches all very closely. I want to talk about the scandalous arrests today. You have seen the list of these unfortunate young people. The young De Chézy, the little Laroque, my nephew Bernard, my little cousin De Landricourt, that is to say the best ... all the valiant!

MOIRANS: You talk about them like soldiers fallen on the field of battle.

DE MÉZIDON: Haven't you noticed that nowadays the street is becoming a field of battle?

MOIRANS: This fact is not very new, only up to now you would have blushed to commit yourself on this issue.

DE MÉZIDON: Is it our fault if the wretch forces us there? But the question is not there. It's necessary, my dear Deputy, that you take the responsibility to put the question to the government.

MOIRANS: So, these brawlers interest you? You find there is heroism in going to spit on the bust of poor Kellner?[30]

DE MÉZIDON: Don't speak to me about that senile decrepit one.

MOIRANS: ... and shouting like wild beasts, and blackening an eye of a policeman?

DE MÉZIDON: Would you be touched by what happened to the police now? I myself maintain that these brawlers, as you say, they are the brave ones, they do not have any choice.

MOIRANS: Silence would be better than such a puerile demonstration.

DE MÉZIDON: Puerile! Puerile! It doesn't prevent them from being tightly locked up at the present hour.

MOIRANS: I remember having heard you cheer about the comfort of the prisons of the Republic.

DE MÉZIDON: It seems however that we are not as well off as all that. And then that is not the question. Everyone is free to express his opinions, our enemies claim that at least.

MOIRANS: You are going to quote Veuillot, I see where this is going.

---

30 An active Zionist. A professor of English and writer of books about the English language as well as the writings of Shakespeare. He was of Austrian origin.

DE MÉZIDON: I don't know who that is. (Moirans hardly conceals a smile.) Besides, you will no longer doubt when you learn that these come-dians have arrested Father Guénard.

MOIRANS: Father Guénard? The one who was pastor of Saint Anselm's?

DE MÉZIDON: (*triumphantly*) Exactly.

MOIRANS: Well! Nothing gave me so much pleasure as that arrest.

DE MÉZIDON: Huh! You rejoice that we have locked up this holy man?

MOIRANS: Holy man! Let me laugh; an old trickster who believes in nothing.

DE MÉZIDON: Permit me to ...

MOIRANS: Who having had in the Church the nastiest stories, those that one prefers to hush up, threw himself headlong into politics—what politics! This is the man who every Friday writes articles in *The Standard*, articles that he doesn't sign, in order to denounce the private villainies of the adversary.

DE MÉZIDON: One fights as one can.

MOIRANS: ... the man who meets with domestics and pays them with cash for their gossip; the man who hears the confessions of the mistresses of our good society men, when they think they are dying, and extorts from them in exchange for a reduction in purgatory, the confidences which he publishes the next day. And they arrested that nasty monkey? Long live the Republic!

DE MÉZIDON: (*vexed*) Perhaps your attitude will change when you learn that those in high places are very troubled by the arrest of the Reverend Father. The canon of Saint Francis, with whom I spoke, just a little earlier, confided to me that the Bishop has the greatest esteem for Father Guénard, and that they are counting on you to obtain ...

MOIRANS: On me? On me? But this is madness! Does it concern me? Is it for me to release Father Guénard? What does that mean?

DE MÉZIDON: Given the credit that you have at your disposal in the Chamber...

MOIRANS: You imagine that I would get a vote of reversal? You are naïve.

DE MÉZIDON: (*rising*) It's enough. I didn't expect, I admit it, that a request so natural might be rebuffed in such a manner. And I will not be the only one to be surprised at the brutal way in which you have rebuffed it.

MOIRANS: (*calming down a little*) But you must understand that I cannot unite with these fanatics.

DE MÉZIDON: That word is inappropriate.

MOIRANS: There is nothing, you understand me, nothing in common between myself and these rogues.

DE MÉZIDON: I thought, sir, that there was between you and those that you call "these rogues"—two ties: the love of France and the love of God.

MOIRANS: The love of God!

DE MÉZIDON: These valiant ones (*Moirans has a wry smile; De Mézidon frowns*), these valiant ones are the very humble servants of the Church, sir, it is important not to forget that. The Church approves their zeal.

MOIRANS: If you are talking about a few fanatical priests ...

DE MÉZIDON: Mr. Deputy, you are forgetting yourself; you are treating the Bishop as a fanatical priest. I wish not to retain any memory of these words, and to attribute them to I know not what madness of an hour ago.

MOIRANS: You are free to do so. (*A silence.*)

DE MÉZIDON: And now that we have both calmed down again, explain to me, my dear Deputy, what has come over you. Do you know that an opponent would not have spoken to me differently?

MOIRANS: An opponent of what?

DE MÉZIDON: You understand me quite well. Admit that during one of your whims as your friends note sometimes with you, you take pleasure in speaking as would your worst enemies. Admit that you enjoy fooling us from time to time about your true feelings by your sudden ill- tempered outbursts.

MOIRANS: What do you know about my feelings?

DE MÉZIDON: About your true convictions, if you prefer.

MOIRANS: What do you know of my convictions? (*A silence; crossing his arms*). So you pretend to know me, you pretend to lock me inside the four walls of your dogmatism?

PETER: (*entering*) Pardon.

MOIRANS: (*to Peter*) Stay, my friend. (*To De Mézidon*) You make the claim of taking the measure of my thought and tell me: "Here you overdo it, there you are not sincere." What do you know about me but what I really wanted to reveal? Do you pride yourself on possessing a special insight?

DE MÉZIDON: Come now. It is better that I get going.

MOIRANS: My poor Mr. De Mézidon, you've lost a few illusions about the simplicity of my nature.

DE MÉZIDON: I thought on entering here, and I still believe, that you take a strange pleasure in confusing, yes sir, in confusing your friends.

MOIRANS: Well! Dear sir, do continue to believe it, it's all the same to me.

DE MÉZIDON: Allow me.

MOIRANS: I didn't wish to hurt you; I apologize for what I just said. No hard feelings, right?

DE MÉZIDON: Why of course! (*Handshakes; De Mézidon goes out.*)

Act One: Scene Thirteen

Moirans, Peter

MOIRANS: Excuses for this idiot, it's of no consequence, and it gave him so much pleasure!

PETER: I only wanted to tell you, sir that your housekeeper is doing really well, there is no longer any concern.

MOIRANS: My friend listen ... You must have been stupefied just now on hearing me.

PETER: That does not concern me. (*He wants to go.*)

MOIRANS: Stay, you do not have to be so discreet. My friend, have a seat.

PETER: I feel that I do not have the right to listen. At this moment you desire to confide in me ... It relieves at first, yes. And then afterwards one regrets. No, I know now that there is a veil that covers a part of your thoughts, I'm asking you not to lift it.

MOIRANS: (*astonished*) Why?

PETER: I cannot explain it. It seems to me that we must not be intimate. I wouldn't understand you. I think that I am not intelligent enough you see. Often, I've already sensed that your real life was very secret and that one day it would take your fancy to … But one must not, I assure you.

MOIRANS: My friend, I do not understand you.

PETER: It's that a similar thing happened to me once; I confided in someone whom I thought worthy of my secrets. I opened my heart to him, my thoughts, everything … I recall it was a night abroad, the weather was beautiful. I spoke for a long time; and when I fell silent I saw that he had not understood; that hurt very much.

MOIRANS: I feel however that you will understand. It's quite ridiculous what I'm going to tell you … a man already mature to a young man like you … I wish you had pity on me, Peter. I am very much alone, I am horribly alone. All those people who were here earlier—you didn't see them— they are so distant, and one must speak to them as if they were very close. One cannot depict, you see, what that solitude can be; there are moments when I know that I am nasty; and then I blame myself; and then it seems to me that I have a right to be so. We do not know what we should be proud of. It seems to me sometimes that I am like a man who would have great treasures and who would like to find what is the most precious; and at each object pulled out he tells himself that that's not it and that that is worth nothing. Yes, I am speaking to you, and perhaps you are not even listening to what I am saying, but it's good to talk … I promise you that I will not seek to know if you have understood. Our actions and our words fall into the unknown, always.

PETER: And people think you are happy!

MOIRANS: There are times when I think myself happy; I don't know: perhaps I am happy. Even this uneasiness that you do not know—this fever—I would not be able to do without it; it's like the pulse of intelligence.

PETER: But why … why this uneasiness? You who have the fortune to have a faith for which you fight, for which you give yourself? This fortune, ah! If I had had it! You have a program, you have a party. You are not amorphous like us who barely know what we want, what we believe. You are enviable, ah! How much so! ... if I had had all that, do you imagine that I would have accepted this lamentable makeshift job of caring for bodies, of recovering motor functions? Our swinging to and fro, our uncertainties, you have not known them.

MOIRANS: I have not known them? My poor child do you believe it? But the life of my thought has only been a dance on a tightrope with vertigo from all sides, the vertigo of freedom always in peril ... So you believe me dependent on a party, like a stone embedded in a wall? And this faith that you attribute to me, for me it would be a natural gift, a property ... I would believe as one digests? You think that? You imagine that my mind has never traveled to the dangerous peaks, toward the other side of the valley, there where all that we affirmed seems insane, where all that we deny seems plausible?

PETER: You think that you possess the truth—whether you have fought or not to acquire it.

MOIRANS: What truth? That of yesterday, that of today, that of tomorrow, or the hypothetical and vague law that connects them? You think me mesmerized by I don't know what childish creed in which all the wisdom of past and future centuries is condensed? Alas! Blessed are those who have not had the idea of history, happy those who have not meditated on the banks of some river the "always changing" (πα τα   ) of the ancient sage. Everything slips away, and ideas themselves, they are no longer these eternal models, these unchangeable types toward which every well born soul endeavored and which smiled indulgently on its efforts. Everything passes.

PETER: How can you act, if you believe that?

MOIRANS: Would you wish then that I remain in inert and desperate contemplation of eternal becoming, in this headlong flight toward some unknown nothingness, we don't know what wretched eclecticism, where all dreams, where all thoughts will be annihilated in an ultimate chaos? Tell me, would you prefer that?

PETER: Every day you affirm; how can you affirm if you do not believe?

MOIRANS: What is belief if not the self-same affirmation?

PETER: I cannot follow you. You even deny the truth.

MOIRANS: What is the truth of a belief? Do you think that we believe in God and in immortality as one believes in the inhabitants of Mars? Do you think that to the privileged eyes of faith, the gates of heaven open, and that unfolds before them I don't know what land of eternal rosy light where angels billow about? ... (*With contempt*) For the humble, yes, for the simple, maybe it is that; perhaps among the disadvantaged souls, and weak intellects, hope hatches these mirages; perhaps they are situated in the kingdom of heaven, beyond our world, in some unthinkable and nonetheless spatial place ... (*a silence*). But on the rigid peaks no vision flowers. True faith overcomes the illusion of the object; it knows that there is no tangible rock against which high thoughts collide. Our thoughts are in themselves their only reality; they refuse to suspend themselves on the forbidden terraces of a world.

PETER: Where you see a victory I only see a fallacy; and I think of those who live by your words, of those who come to warm themselves at the contact of a faith which they ascribe to you and which you do not possess.

MOIRANS: You do not have the right to speak like that. To believe is not to know, it is not to imagine, it is not even to assume: it is to love. No doubt there are images which pass in the depths of a darkened room and which human enthusiasm acclaims at the passage, like excited children at magic lantern shows. But among these images, if there are some ignoble ones which are made for the music hall, there are others which are divine and which deserve to be worshiped. They pass like the others and like the others they are vain, and it is a victory to understand them; there is not one of them that best reflects that land beyond the stars toward which our poor dreams arise; there is not one of them which expresses as a tangible symbol the ultimate sense by which our powerless understanding would summarize the universe. You should love them for themselves, these lovely and fleeting images. Belief is only that: the adhesion of the whole soul, fervent adhesion to a beautiful dream which one knows to be only a dream.

PETER: But for those who hear you, you know very well that it is something else; you know very well that they do not attach to the terms that you use, this subtle and transposed meaning.

MOIRANS: What can I do? And is it my fault if thoughts do not communicate?

PETER: Admit it then, that you delude souls by this isolation in order to bait them.

MOIRANS: I see that you understand me so poorly! In this faith that is mine, you only see dialectical juggling or the abstract game of my pride; whereas for me it is a requirement and a need ... Often in hours of anguish, I've seen a landscape floating before me ... here, this one just about ... an old city almost asleep while the evening dies. Beyond the river which winds with calm murmur amidst the banks, we glimpse steeples and towers. Everything belongs to the past, to memory, to prayer, and the soul kneels with remorse at the edge of this landscape.

PETER: That is only a lyrical impression ...

MOIRANS: But that may be enough to form a soul. I remember an hour that I spent when I was twelve years old in a village cemetery, the church was dilapidated and the crosses were falling into ruins. I remember that intoxication with death. (*A silence.*)

PETER: It seems to me that I might guess what your life must be now; that's quite right, yes, the dance on a tightrope. The mind cannot free itself of what you call the illusion of the object, any more than the body can free itself of weight. Do not deny it, that at certain hours that old question of right and of wrong asserts itself.

MOIRANS: It's taken me twenty years to reach the point that it no longer assails me.

PETER: You have not triumphed ... Sorry to have to say so ... The fervent adhesion to a dream, you were saying. But you yourself then, don't you realize that there is something else, a reality?

MOIRANS: There are other images that fill me with horror. The millennial ascent with the monkey at the summit, and tomorrow the crowd red amidst the odor of the slaughterhouse ... Because they will come; I am sure of it, more sure than all of them. I can already hear their cries (*He hides his face in his hands.*) To have delayed that if only for an hour, that would be already enough.

PETER: By fighting against it, you yourself confess this dreadful truth, and this millennial ascent against which you are rebelling, can you prevent it from having taken place?

MOIRANS: To have happened! To have to happen! Is that enough in your mind to make a truth? A truth! It would have to be something that could envelop the world and myself! What is a truth which I can overcome by denying it!

PETER: And yet if the crowd stones you, you will be the victim of this truth that you deny?

MOIRANS: Do you believe that faith is proved by brute force? There is more to be of my faith than in the gesture of a crowd against which it can do nothing ... And so, you see, at the moment I was not sincere. Nevertheless it would be that cosmic truth, what would it be worth to me, since I would not have had to choose it? I am among those who have never known how to receive. (*A silence.*)

PETER: Who would dare to judge you? This word makes you smile and you are right. Perhaps my scruples and my terror are only the sign of my weakness ... Perhaps. And yet I don't know. My admiration goes to others that you ... to even those humble ones that you disdain.

MOIRANS: Let's envy them but let us not admire them: they have not experienced the temptations of intelligence, and they are the only ones worth resisting. Those who were still confessing their faith in the agony of the last ordeal, they felt in the flame of the bonfires the freshness of the breezes of the eternal gardens; above the homicidal crowds they heard the singing of the blessed. Mediocre is the courage nourished by such certainties.

PETER: Courage, is it everything?

MOIRANS: Beyond a freedom that is exercised in the absolute, there is only nothingness.

PETER: To your dizzying dance, I think I still prefer my mediocre life, to your sublime dangers my poor risks.

MOIRANS: I haven't tried to convert you, proselytism is hardly my thing. (*He looks past him.*) Pardon: you see, I just feel that you are right; our solitude is in us … What can you think of me? I will never know; you would tell me, your very words on falling in me would become mine … No it's better that you not express what I am reading on your lips. That would be painful, you understand.

PETER: Are you really so alone? Your youngest daughter …

MOIRANS: Clarisse? What do you know? I've hoped, yes … without her, without the joy of seeing her grow and shine, I would have become … I don't know … a poor rag, a wreck of intelligence. But she is so secret, so closed.

PETER: (*moved*) Yes.

MOIRANS: I sense in her such an unknown.

PETER: (*lowering his voice*) You cannot read her. She has no expression in the depths of her eyes. (*Moirans looks at him.*)

CLARISSE: (*entering, very pale*) Father ... Ah! Pardon me.

PETER: (*rising*) Stay, miss.

MOIRANS: What is it?

CLARISSE: It's nothing. I will come back. (*She goes out.*)

PETER: She does not appear strong.

MOIRANS: She's been tired these days.

PETER: (*deeply*) It takes a lot to handle her.

MOIRANS: My friend, look at me. (*Peter turns away his face.*) Why not admit to me that ...

PETER: That would be madness. She is not able to love me. (*He rises.*)

MOIRANS: Why are you leaving?

PETER: I cannot ... I cannot ... (*He goes out*).

Act One: Scene Fourteen

Moirans; then Clarisse

Moirans remains pensive, his chin in his hands; Clarisse, coming back.

CLARISSE: Father, why did you deceive me?

MOIRANS: I didn't deceive you; everything that I told you is true.

CLARISSE: Useless to cover up. Theresa told me everything.

MOIRANS: Despite my prohibition? Ah ... (*he has a violent gesture*).

CLARISSE: You mustn't blame her. I am the one who insisted.

MOIRANS: (*bitterly*) So you didn't believe me?

CLARISSE: I really felt that you didn't tell me everything.

MOIRANS: Then she was despicable enough to tell you ...

CLARISSE: Why shouldn't I know? (*Ardently*) It seems to me that she taught me nothing? And then ... one doesn't have the right to ignore these things ...

MOIRANS: You don't understand that I wanted to preserve you from this contact; I would have loved so much that nothing of that sort might ever touch you. Purity of soul is such a precious thing.

CLARISSE: Is it purity of soul not to understand anything ... and must one wish to go through life without seeing anything? Ah! You did not have to decide in my place; father, you have hurt me, more deeply than I can say.

MOIRANS: You are still very young, it was necessary to decide for you.

CLARISSE: Fortunately soon ... (*Moirans looks at her anxiously*). And now what is going to become of her?

MOIRANS: (*with bitterness*) Did the two of you together discuss her future?

CLARISSE: You say that with such a tone! Father, I've had to ask myself if you were good.

MOIRANS: Have I given you occasion to doubt it?

CLARISSE: It's not about me; father, the spirit of charity, is it in you?

MOIRANS: Spare me this verbiage, you are not a priest.

CLARISSE: I find you changed today (*her eyes fill up with tears*); you have never spoken to me like that.

MOIRANS: My little one, I did not want to hurt you, you well know it ... so she told you she wants a divorce?

CLARISSE: Why do you forbid her to do it?

MOIRANS: You do not know therefore that it is a sin, that marriage is indissoluble?

CLARISSE: Theresa is not a believer, she has told me that.

MOIRANS: But if for the rest of us it is a sin, isn't it our duty to oppose it? (*Clarisse looks at him.*) Why are you looking at me like that?

CLARISSE: I don't know. It's the tone with which you said it.

MOIRANS: By divorcing she incurs damnation. Don't we have the duty ...

CLARISSE: God reads into the depths of hearts; if Theresa has the will to divorce, it doesn't matter whether one forbids her from doing it.

MOIRANS: What you say is childish; ask any priest ... At that rate we'd all be criminals.

CLARISSE: We are all criminals.

MOIRANS: It's understood ... original sin ... but it's not the same thing, that has no relevance.

CLARISSE: Whether she divorces or not, it's just a formality.

MOIRANS: A formality! You don't understand then that if she divorces it will be to remarry!

CLARISSE: Can the indissolubility of marriage still exist for her, if in her heart she denies it?

MOIRANS: With these ideas, no Church would be possible.

CLARISSE: However, father, religion is a thing of the soul ... One would say that it's all the same to you that Theresa doesn't believe, provided that she doesn't divorce. Father, I don't understand you well. Explain to me.

MOIRANS: It's not all the same to me, but I am not able to do anything about it.

CLARISSE: We can pray for her.

MOIRANS: Yes, of course.

CLARISSE: I will pray ... It looks like to you prayer doesn't count.

MOIRANS: But how do you not understand that there is a social aspect of our actions which from a purely human point of view, I am not speaking of God at this moment ...

CLARISSE: And yet, what is the judgment of men?

MOIRANS: With your ideas it is necessary to live in a cloister. (*Clarisse makes a gesture.*) When one lives in society, for me especially who has a situation ...

CLARISSE: My God, what I was afraid of is true; it's because of people's opinions that you oppose Theresa's divorce!

MOIRANS: Childishness again. Do I busy myself about what people will say in general?

CLARISSE: It is not the thought of Theresa's salvation ...

MOIRANS: Theresa's salvation! If I object to her divorce, it is forbidden that my daughter's actions contradict me. It is about me, do you clearly understand the difference?

CLARISSE: I don't want to understand. In my eyes this amounts to the same thing.

MOIRANS: If you do not want to grasp it, it's up to you. (*He goes out.*)

CLARISSE: (*alone*) Now I know why it has to be ... And I will not even be Aunt Clarisse. (*She goes out weeping.*)

CURTAIN

ACT TWO

(Same décor)

Act Two: Scene One

Mrs. Moirans; Henry

HENRY: She said to me: "You understand it yourself, Yvonne cannot be the sister-in-law of a divorcee."

MRS. MOIRANS: What did you respond?

HENRY: Nothing. I don't know. I was dumbfounded. I denied it. Let's see, mama, you understand that we must prevent this.

MRS. MOIRANS: But how do we do it my poor child? Theresa has agreed to speak to Father Grandin, they are together at this moment. But to say that I have confidence ...

HENRY: We must speak up. Father should still have enough authority ... Altogether what difference can it make to Theresa to only be separated? She cannot still harbor illusions about her chances of remarriage.

MRS. MOIRANS: Henry!

HENRY: I would say much more ... I am in a state! ... I was so happy.

MRS. MOIRANS: I understand that it must be hard for you to give up this charming child.

HENRY: But I do not accept for a minute that I must give her up, not a minute, you hear me. There are ways of doing this. Mrs. de Lucé told me she would come to see you.

MRS. MOIRANS (*fearfully*): She is going to come!

HENRY: Look into it together.

MRS. MOIRANS: Speak to your sister.

HENRY: When Theresa has something in her head ... besides, it's a family trait!

MRS. MOIRANS: Unfortunately!

HENRY: Here is Mrs. De Lucé, I beg you, find something. My happiness depends on it. (*He goes out.*)

Act Two: Scene Two

Mrs. Moirans, Mrs. de Lucé

MRS. DE LUCÉ: My poor friend ... so it's true? I was still hoping! This unfortunate child has strayed to that point ... and yet her husband is a charming man (*upon a gesture of Mrs. Moirans*). Yes, of course, I can well imagine ... but in the end all men are the same. If we don't close our eyes ... It's a great misfortune that she has no children. These nasty ideas would not even come to mind.

MRS. MOIRANS: (*slumping*) Father Grandin is trying to convince her at this moment ...

MRS. DE LUCÉ: Father is a saintly man; but he doesn't have what it takes for that. Ah! If it were Father Lemoyne or Father Guénard, that martyr! ... Those men know how to persuade. I remember, in a very sad circumstance, Father Guénard had an influence on my life ... That man, when he spoke of the future life ... one believed oneself to be already in paradise. But let's not stray from the point. We must absolutely, you hear me, my dear friend, we must absolutely avoid this terrible misfortune.

Henry must have told you ... we would have to withdraw ... and my poor little daughter ...

MRS. MOIRANS: Henry is very unhappy.

MRS. DE LUCÉ: I tell you quite frankly, I don't know how Yvonne would bear this disappointment. It would be necessary to drag her again to the thermal spas ... we must at all costs prevent that. Do you want me to say a word to your daughter?

MRS. MOIRANS: (*hesitating*) I thank you, but I don't know if ...

MRS. DE LUCÉ: She's not a stone nevertheless. The idea of ruining the happiness of her brother, of poisoning your existence ...

MRS. MOIRANS: Theresa is highly embittered.

MRS. DE LUCÉ: That's not a reason. And yet, if one cannot decide, there is perhaps another way ... I was thinking about it while coming here.

OIRANS: What is it?

MRS. DE LUCÉ: Annulment.

MRS. MOIRANS: However ...

MRS. DE LUCÉ: I assure you; it's something to think about.

MRS. MOIRANS: After three years of marriage ...

MRS. DE LUCÉ: The Princess de Rouvray obtained an annulment by the Rome tribunal after four years of marriage.

MRS. MOIRANS: But perhaps it was different, and then it's an important family.

MRS. DE LUCÉ: You know that my brother was a school classmate of Cardinal Scacchi. I am placing everything at your disposal ... Think about it. The case is exactly the same as that of the Princess de Rouvray; there were no children. Think carefully...

MRS. MOIRANS: I ask nothing better, but all the same we cannot ... Reverend Father!

Act Two: Scene Three

TMrs. Morains and Father Grandin present

MRS. MOIRANS: Reverend Father, were you able to obtain anything?

FATHER GRANDIN: I have just spent some very painful moments with Mrs. Naudier, as a priest and as a friend.

MRS. DE LUCÉ: Reverend Father prefers to remain alone with you, dear friend.

REVEREND GRANDIN: Madam, don't think ...

MRS. DE LUCÉ: Yes, it's quite natural moreover. I will come back. (*She goes out.*)

Act Two: Scene Four

Moirans; Father Grandin

FATHER GRANDIN: Poor mother!

MRS. MOIRANS: So, we are not able to hope for anything?

FATHER GRANDIN: Your daughter will not hear of it. In vain I appealed to all those Christian virtues: faith, patience, resignation ... I did feel that for her it was all just words. The one who humiliated her carries a terrible responsibility before God, Madam, for he is the author of this disaffection for religion which alas, only appears too obvious to me. This man believes in nothing, and for several weeks at the beginning of their union, when he had the confidence of your daughter, it pleased him to uproot belief in her heart.

MRS. MOIRANS: Do you think it's that, Reverend Father? I don't know, but I would have thought rather that it was misfortune ...

FATHER GRANDIN: Misfortune draws us closer to God, madam; it is not at the time when the soul is crushed under the weight of misfortune that she frees herself of all religion.

MRS. MOIRANS: I would have thought however ...

FATHER GRANDIN: I know it is as I say. (*Pause*) In vain I begged her to wait until our prayers have borne fruit; in vain I exhorted her to resume, before deciding anything, those regular practices that for a long time she had neglected. In vain I painted for her in the most vivid colors, the despair into which an entire family will be plunged through her fault. The spirit of pride, the spirit of revolt is still in her, and I fear that it will take some hard lessons to drive it out of her heart.

MRS. MOIRANS: My God, all this is terrible; yet we never neglected her religious instruction— and she was the easiest of my three children.

FATHER GRANDIN: Take courage, afflicted mother; divine grace makes its way by very secret pathways, and perhaps, at the very moment when you are lamenting, an event is in preparation that will bring joy back to your disconsolate house.

MRS. MOIRANS: What do you mean, Reverend Father?

FATHER GRANDIN: I cannot speak more clearly, because it is a secret that doesn't belong to me; the person who has confided it to me desires that for some time yet, it not be spread.

MRS. MOIRANS: Who are you talking about? Reverend Father, give me an answer. You have just created a new concern in me. It's about Clarisse, isn't it? Tell me everything, I am her mother, I have the right to know. Pity, Father. My life has been difficult, I assure you, you cannot imagine how much.

FATHER GRANDIN: Perhaps after all I should satisfy your quite legitimate curiosity. Yes, it's indeed about Miss Clarisse; she has just confided in me that she has the intention of taking the veil.

MRS. MOIRANS: Clarisse, in the convent!

FATHER GRANDIN: Happy woman! Even happier mother! While your husband by his eloquence will make the cause of God triumph, your daughter, by the efficaciousness of her prayers and her virtues ...

MRS. MOIRANS: Forgive me, Reverend Father, but it's so unexpected ... so alarming.

FATHER GRANDIN: (*hearing himself speak*) You see, it was too early to despair, divine providence has not forgotten you; at the very moment when it seems to be abandoning you, it has taken care by a glorious favor ...

MRS. MOIRANS: Reverend Father, are you sure that it is happiness? Me, I don't know, I am only a poor woman, and it is so hard to think that she wants to renounce life ...

FATHER GRANDIN: What you call life is only vanity. Consider that on wings she will rise above this world and its miseries, that in this life she will live another life ... (*in a different tone*). Do you think then that I do not understand your agitation and that I do not sympathize at all? Your anguish is only too natural; but you owe it to yourself, you owe it to your

Christian soul to overcome it. Soon you will experience a kind of solemn joy at the thought that among so many others, your child has been selected.

MRS. MOIRANS: (*who has not listened*) And then ... pardon Reverend Father ... why has she never told me anything? No one has ever had confidence in me, and that seems so cruel.

FATHER GRANDIN: It was necessary so that no human voice might come to trouble her holy meditation. Up to these last few days, she has been waiting, she told me so herself. She was not sure of having heard the call, she had not yet recognized it with that infallible certainty with which the heart of men welcomes the word of God.

MRS. MOIRANS: Up to these last few days, you say; but then if it was under the influence of what Theresa told her ... Think about it, Reverend Father, could it be a whim?

FATHER GRANDIN: Can you believe, madam that I was not concerned? The noble child assured me that already for years she felt growing inside her the hope to be one day the spouse of Our Lord.

MRS. MOIRANS: For years! And we have suspected nothing! It's not possible.

Act Two: Scene Five

The same characters; Clarisse

MRS. MOIRANS: My child, what Reverend Father tells me is true, you are thinking of entering a convent?

CLARISSE: (*to Reverend Father*) What have you told her?

FATHER GRANDIN: Your mother was worrying. I did not believe it my right to leave her in this anguish.

CLARISSE: I have not yet said anything to my father.

MRS. MOIRANS: Clarisse!

CLARISSE: Reverend Father, why have you told her? She was to learn it only from me. (*A silence.*)

MRS. MOIRANS: My child, have you reflected well about what the life of a religious is? Think about all that you will have to leave!

CLARISSE: Let it be, mama, all that is already behind me.

MRS. MOIRANS: Do you understand what it is? ... You are not even listening to me. My God, what have I done that my own children treat me like a stranger?

CLARISSE: Pardon, mama; but on the path that I wish to take, one has to walk alone.

FATHER GRANDIN (*in a low voice to Mrs. Moirans*): Divine grace is in her; you see what certainty shines in her eyes.

MRS. MOIRANS: Perhaps you have chosen the better way; one sees so many terrible things in life; illnesses ... disasters; look at your sister ... and yet I cannot ... it seems that I do not have the right ... besides your father would not want it.

CLARISSE: Why wouldn't he want it?

MRS. MOIRANS: I don't know, I feel that he would not want it.

FATHER GRANDIN: Allow me, madam, to believe on the contrary that Mr. Moirans will deeply feel the divine favor with which your family is favored. (*Moirans enters at this moment. Silence.*)

Act Two: Scene Six

The same characters; Moirans

MOIRANS: Good evening, Father Grandin. What's the matter? Why did you all fall silent when I entered?

FATHER GRANDIN: We are waiting, Mr. Deputy, with a very lively emotion ...

MRS. MOIRANS: Roger, just imagine ... no, I cannot ... (*she breaks into sobs*).

MOIRANS: What is happening? (*to Clarisse*) why are you so pale, my sweet?

FATHER GRANDIN: When you know, you will find her paleness quite natural. Your noble child has resolved to take the veil.

MOIRANS: What does that mean? Clarisse in the convent?

MRS. MOIRANS: (*to Clarisse*) You see.

MOIRANS: But all in all it is demented! In the convent! Why? (*Clarisse has a pained movement.*)

MRS. MOIRANS: Now you realize that this is not possible ... think about what it would be for us ... losing you ... to see you give up getting married ... of becoming a mother ... think ... if Henry doesn't have children ... one does not enter the cloister without reason.

FATHER GRANDIN: Allow me to remind you, madam, that grace is stronger than all human reason and that it is taking place.

MRS. MOIRANS: Roger, why don't you speak?

MOIRANS: (*briskly*) Leave me alone with her.

MRS. MOIRANS: Control yourself, I entreat you.

FATHER GRANDIN: Think, Mr. Deputy that heavy, quite heavy, is the responsibility that you are going to assume.

MOIRANS: (*harshly*) I assume it entirely and without hesitation. (*Father and Mrs. Moirans go out.*)

Act Two: Scene Seven

Clarisse; Moirans

MOIRANS: Let's see, my sweetheart, tell me who has been able to put this idea in your head? I promise you I will remain calm, I was at first overcome ... Who is it?

CLARISSE: (*firmly unresponsive*) I cannot tell you.

MOIRANS: You won't deny that someone has put pressure on you? Is it reverend father? ... No, I do not think him capable of it; he is not strong enough for that. But who then? (*He thinks*) ... I think I know. It's the aftermath of what your sister has told you. Had I not truly foreseen that this revelation would be disastrous? You revolted against life, you also thought that this would compensate; one divorced, the other in the convent: this balances. Come now my little one, acknowledge that things happened like that? (*With a great sadness.*) So then, it's over, you no longer trust me? However at this moment I am calm, I am in control of myself. Ah well, I will only ask you to wait a few days before deciding anything, you understand, I am sure that in a few days you will see things differently.

CLARISSE: And me, I am sure that my resolve is unwavering.

MOIRANS: So be it. But then what harm could it do to wait ... since nothing will be changed in a few days? That should be all the same to you?

CLARISSE: Father, I swear to you that you are mistaken. I have had the desire to be a religious for years.

MOIRANS: It's not possible. I never knew anything.

CLARISSE: For long years, but it was only in these last months that I felt how imperious was this vocation (*he wants to speak*); Father, I beg you, do not interrupt me. I must already make such an effort to talk. These are things so difficult to express. It's in these last months that I've felt this kind of … (*she hesitates*) embrace, that I heard this kind of call.

MOIRANS: These are words from a novel, this cannot be spontaneous.

CLARISSE: All this is then so foreign to you?

MOIRANS: I will no longer interrupt you.

CLARISSE: It's only in these last months that I saw life fleeing before me like a boat seen by the one who just landed … I cannot explain this otherwise … This does not mean to say that men and things have become indifferent to me. I have often cried during the night, thinking that I will not have children, and even yesterday … This means that I've felt that all this didn't concern me; that I was destined to know nothing of it.

MOIRANS: Destined; what is this fatalism?

CLARISSE: I am not reasoning; I am limiting myself to state what I have felt.

MOIRANS: You believe it; but in reality, in all that you describe there is nothing or almost nothing that would be feeling, there is only the imagination.

CLARISSE: I do not understand what you mean.

MOIRANS: It matters little (*in a different tone*); but you won't deny that the conversation with your sister has made an impression on you, encouraged you.

CLARISSE: Before having heard her I knew; afterward I understood; especially ... (*she stops*).

MOIRANS: What were you going to say?

CLARISSE: Especially after the conversation that I had with you.

MOIRANS: With me? About this unfortunate one? (*gesture indicating he is talking about Theresa*)

CLARISSE: It seemed to me that I would have to pray only for her (*the face of Moirans contracts*). And if you knew, father! If there is a man in the world who has made me what I am! ...

MOIRANS: Well?

CLARISSE: That man is you. And it's because of that that I still want to believe that I didn't understand you yesterday. Do you remember our walks every morning during the summer months, when I was still a little girl?

MOIRANS: Yes.

CLARISSE: You remember that convent of Carmelites that we saw there in the forest, along the river. On the way back I was always tired and to distract me you talked to me about the life led by the nuns, you used to describe their occupations, their joys, you boasted to me about the peace that always reigns in monasteries. I did not seem to listen.

MOIRANS: And you were listening overmuch.

CLARISSE: We looked from afar at the little cemetery with all its tombstones exactly alike.

MOIRANS: It's true, I can see again the big gray house with its tile roof.

CLARISSE: It was on that day that for the first time we really talked about death.

MOIRANS: We've often talked about it since.

CLARISSE: You recall that at one time I was very fearful of death, I even dreamed often that I was buried alive, and I woke up screaming.

MOIRANS: I remember all that.

CLARISSE: What the pastor said never calmed me down, but you ...

MOIRANS: Well then ...

CLARISSE: It is to this convent that I want to go; the river is limpid and murmuring; and one must wake up happy there.

MOIRANS: So then it would be me ...

CLARISSE: Father, I've told you—there is no human explanation for what I have resolved, but if it were necessary to name a man ...

MOIRANS: It would be me? (*Hiding his face in his hands.*) My God, why?

CLARISSE: I recall that one day we witnessed the departure of a novice; the mother was crying—and I was surprised and you said: "We must envy them."

MOIRANS: I said that!

CLARISSE: You did not suspect that your words were resonating in me so deeply.

MOIRANS: Don't repeat that to me. I feel that I cannot resist this idea.

(*A silence.*) It's true, I wanted you pious, I could not bear the thought that you would not be making the eternal gestures before the great spectacles of the faith—but I didn't want you mystical. Why must it be that the shadow of a life stretches so far into the unknown? Why do we not at least benefit from the solitude in which we live and will die? But you are wrong; those who made you, they are your mother and her friends, all those devotees ...

CLARISSE: Father, you know well it is not.

MOIRANS: (*with bewilderment*) I must believe that it is them.

CLARISSE: I have never seen you like this: how can you be unhappy that I was elected? For I was elected, father, I felt the breath of divine election pass over me, and I trembled, I implored that it might be another and not I ... but I heard the inflexible voice that answered: "You, yourself, and not another." Think, father, from that moment I follow, and I can no longer die.

MOIRANS: Listen: I was wrong just now, we must not wait, not even one day. You will leave; if necessary I will leave with you. We will travel. Above all, you must forget. In other places, before other landscapes ... You know nothing of life; believe me, there is enough in it to satisfy all needs, enough to satisfy all aspirations.

CLARISSE: Father, spare me these words; all this sounds so hollow for me now; I only know one exigency and one aspiration, and there is nothing in what you call life that can satisfy it; because that life is death.

MOIRANS: I do not want to hear in your mouth this mystical jargon. Life, you do not understand then that it is activity—all activity, even that of thought; life is all that you still do not yet know, even love.

CLARISSE: The only love that does not deceive ...

MOIRANS: Do you believe then that it doesn't deceive? The God that you want to serve is a capricious lover; you will know hours of drought in which the soul hypnotizes itself on formulas in order to try to open within itself dried up sources; you will know times when you feel emptied of tenderness and faith; you will know ...

CLARISSE: All that I foresee; this life would not attract me if it were not a life of struggles; the path of salvation is that of the greatest dangers.

MOIRANS: There is only one danger, and it's one over which we do not triumph. You will feel your fervor dulled in the monotony of hours eternally the same, your soul will stiffen into the routine of habit; and at first you will hear it, your poor stifled soul, crying out for this life which you will have frustrated; and then little by little it will grow quiet, it will become accustomed to it. Habit, you see, is the terrible enemy over which you will not triumph; and it is habit which is death. Carmelite, my poor child? I evoke what will be your poor pale face in ten years— greenish like a flower in a cave, with those big eyes which will not yet be entirely dimmed and which will try to smile; I evoke the visits more and more rare; one comes without knowing entirely why, because there is nothing to say in this big house where nothing ever happens, and after ten minutes, you have to talk about the weather; and the visits will space themselves like those that one makes to the dead; one only comes on birthdays.

CLARISSE: Father, it's false, you don't know ...

MOIRANS: You think one can flee from life; but no; life takes vengeance on those who want to avoid it; it pursues them into the refuge even in places which they believe to be protected from its attacks. You do not know the petty resentments that still ferment in those unfortunate souls; in vain have they tried to empty them, in vain have they thought to silence in them all the voices of the world: they only hear better in the silence all the whispers, all the complaints, that the big voice of life would have covered. Go on, the peace of convents only exists for those who have never lived there.

CLARISSE: You yourself in the past ...

MOIRANS: I ought not to remember my words of long ago. My child, be strong, be courageous; do not be afraid of life; it is good to those who know how to look it in the face; whatever the tragedies that the day reserves for us, they are worth more than the terrors that burden us at night ... Clarisse, the night is not a refuge.

CLARISSE: You do not understand, I am not looking for a refuge. I am not fleeing from the struggle, I want it. Temptations do not scare me, I would not go to the convent if they did not give me an appointment. Like a storm on a summit, the struggle is more terrible at the peaks of life ...

MOIRANS: (*surprised*) What do you mean?

CLARISSE: At the summits of life there is only room for prayer and meditation. The value of life has no other yardstick than the fervor which animates it. Father, I am not looking for rest but turmoil. It seems that I feel now as I have never felt; you might say it is your presence that tears these words from me and yet they were in me; you would say that my soul ignites like yours, yet it is already illuminated. Father, reassure yourself, I do not want that rest in which the soul immobilizes itself in poses of ecstasy and gestures of adoration, I do not want that peace in which hearts get bogged down like in the sand; no, the life toward which I want to go is other, it's a life of combat, and the certainties are rising like victories; the prayers do not follow one another in a rosary that the soul recites mechanically, they shoot up like jets of flame in a fervent chapel.

MOIRANS: Clarisse, I find you at last! ...

CLARISSE: And it seems that I find myself too; from the depths of the infinite a voice calls me—and it is my own.

MOIRANS: My child, my child: your thought is born at this hour and it is the daughter of my thought. As in a symphony a melody gives birth to another melody which reinforces it and transforms it, your soul renews my soul ... This hour that I have summoned in the silence of the night has arrived. I was alone and now we are two. As the sound of a stream to a thirsty traveler, your presence has revealed itself to my solitude. Blessed be this childish dream in which you have lived, since it is in it that I have just found you: I know well how to pull you away from its evil spell.

CLARISSE: No, you will not be able to any more, father, and your words are in vain. I am in possession of myself at last, you will no longer be able to tear me away from myself.

MOIRANS: Clarisse, do you remember the little cemetery where rest those who are dead without having lived. Think of the agony of those last minutes, when life unfolds entirely to the eyes in a twilight haze, and one knows that it is all spent and that there is no more to do but to say farewell. Think about the idea that it's too late, and that the game is played for all eternity, and there is no more starting again. To die, Clarisse, to die not as an old man who knows and is able to remember, but as a child who has never seen anything and for whom memory is like a blank page! Death, Clarisse! ...

CLARISSE: (*in a vibrant voice*) From this moment I accept it, I welcome it, and I clamor for it.

MOIRANS: No one has the right to speak like that. It is unmentionable and thought stops when the shadow of death passes.

CLARISSE: Father, admit it: you are afraid.

MOIRANS: (*in a low voice*) Yes, it's true, I am afraid. Do not judge; this fear, one cannot know it at your age. But you will see when you have lived ... one really has the feeling that one is spending one's life—and that in the end nothing remains. At your age one thinks one is inexhaustible, and then ... (*he makes a sorrowful gesture*).

CLARISSE: (*in a low voice, deeply disturbed*) Your words are not those of a Christian. (*A silence.*) Father, who are you?

MOIRANS: I thought I knew, I no longer know. But I cannot let you go this way in the night; now especially that I have discovered you and that I feel you so close ...

CLARISSE: You have no right to speak to me like this. There is a gulf between us.

MOIRANS: Child! While you were expressing your ardor just now, there was in your voice ...

CLARISSE: Do not try to mislead me, I see so clearly now why you do not understand.

MOIRANS: You said so yourself: nothing has the value of fervor; what does it matter what the images are that translate it for us?

CLARISSE: They are not images, they are realities, the only realities. Your face would not have become so pale at only the thought of death if it was only an image for you ...

MOIRANS: You are mistaken: death is only an image, but it is frightening for those who draw near to it. Your youthful fantasy can only see a reality there because it imagines behind it some worlds and some lives.

CLARISSE: I will pray that he enlighten you, He who has elected me and I know that my prayers will be heard.

MOIRANS: You are rambling. The bars of our prison are well sealed; we live there alone from birth to death, there is no human or divine thought that can force open the doors. I have been crazy enough to sometimes distress myself over it; senseless! The pain of living would be without remedy if it were in the power of a thought to act on my thinking.

CLARISSE: (*gently*) Father, God is Love, and in love thoughts communicate.

MOIRANS: Alas! Love itself only pursues a phantom, and one that it has created itself. Clarisse, if there is some passageway from this phantom to your being, listen to my supplication; I want to forget this wisdom which renders one nasty; forget even that I am not as you have believed.

CLARISSE: I will not be able to.

MOIRANS: It's only a man who is speaking to you, a man who tomorrow will be an old man. You must take pity on me, Clarisse. The God in which you believe cannot order you to hurt me.

CLARISSE: I can only heal you in Him and through Him.

MOIRANS: I am not asking you to heal me, understand. I do not wish to become like the simple; I've been able to wish sometimes, in hours of anguish in which it seemed that I couldn't bear my thoughts, and a vertigo was drawing me down toward what they call the faith of the humble, which is only a deception.

CLARISSE: Father, that faith is mine.

MOIRANS: It is no longer yours. You do not believe like the humble, Clarisse, because they fear temptation, and you seek it. There is no horizon that you can open to me; for I am at the extreme promontory, you see, and beyond it one can no longer think any more.

CLARISSE: You think yourself at the end, and you are only at the beginning.

MOIRANS: Wait a few years when you have joined me ...

CLARISSE: I will never come to your point, I would rather ... (*she is quiet*).

MOIRANS: Do not finish; that day you will have joined me.

CLARISSE: At each one of your words the certainty in me becomes clearer, at each of your words I understand better why I must go there.

MOIRANS: It is no longer Grace which is leading you, since you can reason.

CLARISSE: With words you will always triumph, but ...

MOIRANS: (*enviously*) It's true, you are young, you have the future, and it seems to you that the prayers of your new soul are soaring to a new heaven. But I ... it has been thirty years, you see, and more, that I am meditating with sterility. And I feel rise in me from those words and from those things an insipid and sickening odor, that of some churches on Sunday evening. All that is two thousand years old, there isn't any cry of adoration that hasn't been repeated thousands of times, there isn't a fervent thought which hasn't been reproduced in thousands of souls, each time with that shiver of ecstasy which welcomes revelations. Think of that ... Why is it necessary that I try to communicate to you this great disgust that I feel sometimes? Why?

CLARISSE: Do not evoke the past, because these memories which were so dear to me have become intolerable; I know now what a hideous comedy you have acted; do not wait for me to save you: father, I am in horror of you. To have done for twenty years all the gestures of religion, to have thrown around you the seeds of faith with full hand, all with this great void in the heart, ah! It's not too much for a life to wash clean all that.

MOIRANS: I refuse your prayers, I reject them.

CLARISSE: But He will not reject them.

MOIRANS: A little human pity ...

CLARISSE: What you call human pity would be the worst of abandonment.

MOIRANS: Well! If you pray to him, this God of your puerile dreams, beg him to send me deliverance soon; pray for my death.

CLARISSE: One only prays for births. (*She goes out.*)

Act Two: Scene Eight

Moirans, then Mrs. Moirans

MRS. MOIRANS: Well, what has happened? (*He does not answer.*) Roger, I have the right all the same to know what she said to you. I see by your face that you have obtained nothing. Roger, answer me.

MOIRANS: (*harshly*) What do you want to know?

MRS. MOIRANS: Don't speak to me like that; I feel that I will not be able to bear it. Life is too difficult, it pushes hard behind me. Father said that it was a great happiness, but I cannot think like that. Roger, I ask you as a favor, tell me what you said to one another.

MOIRANS: Well! She is walled in by her dream; she does not want to hear anything, and no one will obtain anything from her.

MRS. MOIRANS: So you yourself have obtained nothing! And yet you had all her confidence, you, she used to listen to you ...

MOIRANS: One moment I thought that I would be able to reason with her, but no, she is already far gone. And it is my fault.

MRS. MOIRANS: I have never seen you so unhappy. If at least that was able to bring us together! Roger! This time we feel the same way. After all these bad years, will we finally have this kind of joy?

MOIRANS: Of suffering together?

MRS. MOIRANS: I feel so deeply that we will have to forget all that has separated us; me, I will know how to forget all your hardness and this cruel silence. It will be necessary for us to have each other now; Henry is going to get married.

MOIRANS: And then that one ... (*he makes a gesture of contempt*).

MRS. MOIRANS: Theresa is too independent ...

MOIRANS: You are right. It will be necessary that we suffice one to the other. The evenings will seem long, eh, my poor Louise? What will we find to say to one another? We have the resource of going to bed early.

MRS. MOIRANS: Roger! Can't you say anything better to me?

MOIRANS: (*looking at her attentively*) You look at me as if I were capable of still giving you something, and I have nothing for you. Others slowly make their provisions for the hours of famine, me I have amassed nothing, not even grudges. Louise, be sincere, doesn't it seem comic and pitiful, our history together?

MRS. MOIRANS: My God, what do you mean?

MOIRANS: What is there in common between us? What do we know of one another? Have we really loved each other for one hour, I'm saying one hour?

MRS. MOIRANS: (*with momentum*) Roger, how can you not know that I have loved you?

MOIRANS: (*slowly*) So you have loved me ... yes, and perhaps I believed I loved you also back then before our marriage ... You remember when I stayed from Saturday to Monday in the big room on the second floor? How long ago! Yes, I must have given in to the prestige of that old house and those old people ... you remember the chapel, it seems they store hay there now ... and in the middle of all that you must have appeared in a kind of halo of the past. Yes, I remember an evening, there at the Garancière ... I must have been romantic ... but in the head only, like the rest ...

MRS. MOIRANS: So never, never, there has been nothing for me in your heart that one might simply call love; it was necessary to have the setting of the manor, and then once that setting was eliminated ...

MOIRANS: My poor wife, I have again just hurt you, and this time truly I did not want to. (*A silence.*) It is better to know, you see. When one is like me, one is hardly capable of loving people. One attaches oneself to things, to images, to thoughts. In order to love one would have to be able to forget that one is himself, and I have never been able to do so. And yet, her, I loved her ...

MRS. MOIRANS: You are talking about it in the past.

MOIRANS: (*with distraction*) Her, yes, her alone ...

MRS. MOIRANS: Roger, we will talk about her.

MOIRANS: (*with a bitter laugh*) I would not be able to, and then you would finish by becoming jealous. All women ...

MRS. MOIRANS: What do you know about women?

MOIRANS: In effect, I know nothing. I have perhaps missed life—like all those who talk too much about it. Louise, it's true that it is going to be necessary to get used to holding on to one another. You will ask me if I haven't caught a cold, and I will worry about your neuralgia.

MRS. MOIRANS: You, you have your life, you have politics.

MOIRANS: Big word, small thing; and then, no, I will no longer even have that.

MRS. MOIRANS: Why?

Act Two: Scene Nine

The same characters; Mrs. De Lucé

MRS. DE LUCÉ: Well! My poor friends, I see by your face that Father has obtained nothing. But listen to me, I assure you that all is not hopeless. Father Chanteau, to whom I slipped a word about the matter, reminded me that there exists a case of annulment quite practical ... and given the excellent relations of Mr. Moirans with my lord Bishop ...

MOIRANS: From today forward I am completely disinterested in this case; Theresa can divorce if she wishes, I will not lift a finger to prevent her.

MRS. DE LUCÉ: What?

MRS. MOIRANS: We are upset; you must excuse my husband; just imagine, Clarisse has just announced to us that she is determined to become a Carmelite.

MRS. DE LUCÉ: What are you telling me? You must take good care; young girls sometimes have these headstrong impulses ... It's true that your Clarisse is not the woman for it. But then ... Where is she that I might kiss her? Above all, wait before letting her make a resolution. You remember what happened with the de Sénanges; Alice came back before the novitiate—eight years ago—and she is still not married. But if by chance she persists in her resolution, it would be an asset for you; one would really not be able to refuse ...

MOIRANS: You will excuse me, my dear madam, but I have a migraine, I am going to lie down a bit.

Act Two: Scene Ten

Mrs. Moirans, Mrs. De Lucé

MRS. DE LUCÉ: He seems quite ill ... besides don't you have the feeling that he has been overworked lately? I am sure that a little rest would be necessary for him, in Switzerland, for example. Have you heard talk about the visit made to him by Mr. De Mézidon.

MRS. MOIRANS: No.

MRS. DE LUCÉ: It seems that Mr. Moirans was vexed, and that he made comments which have been repeated, inaccurately, I am certain, and which risk doing him harm. I assure you, my friend, you should get him to take some rest.

Act Two: Scene Eleven

The same characters; Henry

HENRY: Well?

MRS. DE LUCÉ: As I have just told your mother, one will be able to, I think, obtain an annulment, provided that your father is ready to make a personal representation to the Bishop.

HENRY: Why wouldn't he lend himself to it?

MRS. DE LUCÉ: And now I must leave you. Calm yourself, everything will work out. (*She goes out.*)

Act Two: Scene Twelve

Henry, Mrs. Moirans

MRS. MOIRANS: Your father is extremely upset, you must not ask him anything right now, and I rather doubt that he would agree to take this step. Perhaps after all it isn't necessary.

HENRY: Why wouldn't he consent?

MRS. MOIRANS: I cannot precisely say but just a while ago he had words that I didn't understand and that worry me.

HENRY: Mama, you must get him to do it and without delay. You don't know what harm can be done to us by the rumors that are accumulating.

Act Two: Scene Thirteen

The same characters; Moirans

MOIRANS: I've told your mother that I have definitively lost interest in this business.

MRS. MOIRANS: I thought that you had gone to lie down.

MOIRANS: You are making such noise that one cannot be calm one instant.

HENRY: But papa, my happiness …

MOIRANS: There is not a thing in the world, you hear me, about which I could totally care less, than what you call your happiness.

MRS. MOIRANS: Roger! …

MOIRANS: Too bad for him. He will understand for once what I think of him. (*To Henry*) You are only a dressed-up dummy. What is your life? What are your concerns? Those of a leader of cotillions. The garden-party of some, the sporting gymkhana of others, the tea-bridge of a third group, with the sole aim of being mentioned the following day in the *Gaulois* newspaper. Whether you marry or not this silly and titled little girl, you will remain the same, isn't that so? A lazy snob who is disconsolate because he doesn't have the noble title.

MRS. MOIRANS: You are unfair; this child is in love, you know it.

MOIRANS: In love with that doll! Let me laugh.

HENRY: Mama! …

MOIRANS: Now go on your way, both of you; I have to write. (*He sits down to write.*)

MRS. MOIRANS *(to Henry)*: Come.

HENRY: I hate him. (*Mrs. Moirans has a pale and sad smile, they go out; Moirans sits at the table and writes.*)

Act Two: Scene Fourteen

Moirans, then Clarisse

CLARISSE: (*entering*) What are you doing, father?

MOIRANS: I am undoing my life.

CURTAIN

ACT THREE

(The same décor)

Act Three: Scene One

Mrs. Moirans, Father Grandin

MRS. MOIRANS: I cannot tell you anything, Father, I know nothing.

FATHER GRANDIN: But in the end, this letter, did it go out?

MRS. MOIRANS: I don't know.

FATHER GRANDIN: One doesn't resign like that, capriciously; France has need of him. And you do not suspect the reason that may have dictated this determination?

MRS. MOIRANS: No. It cannot be Theresa's divorce since it seems that annulment would be easy to obtain.

FATHER GRANDIN: But then, even so, it couldn't be …

MRS. MOIRANS: It's because of Clarisse, I am sure of it.

FATHER GRANDIN: It's impossible. What probability would there be? … and you say that the Bishop has been announced?

MRS. MOIRANS: Here he is.

Act Three: Scene Two

The same characters; Moirans, Bishop Vielle

MOIRANS: Please enter, Bishop.

MRS. MOIRANS: (*greeting with a low bow*) My lord Bishop.

BISHOP VIELLE: Madam ... Reverend Father, I am glad to see you. (*Greetings*)

MRS. MOIRANS: Bishop, we are going to leave you alone with my husband. (*Mrs. Moirans and Father go out.*)

Act Three: Scene Three

Moirans, Bishop Vielle

MOIRANS: My lord Bishop, give yourself the trouble to sit down ... take this arm chair.

BISHOP VIELLE: Thank you, Mr. Deputy, I will be perfect here. I don't know if it is necessary that I explain my visit to you, because you know better that I the reasons that have motivated it. You are not unaware of the rumors that are circulating on your account; it goes without saying that not for one second have I given them any credence, but I have come to ask you, Mr. Deputy, to kindly refute them publicly. Why? It is hardly necessary for me to tell you. Your situation is such that your friends cannot bear to see attributed to you projects and thoughts incompatible with what one knows of your character.

MOIRANS: Thank you, my lord Bishop, in fact I suspected the reason for your visit. Unfortunately ... (*he stops*). I beg your pardon but I am very tired and can barely tie two ideas together, my thoughts do not respond when I call them ... I cannot accede to your desire.

BISHOP VIELLE: And why is that?

MOIRANS: Because they are telling the truth. My letter of resignation is written; it only remains to be sent. I don't know how the entire city is aware of my projects. It is true that I hardly monitored my words yesterday evening. But I repeat to you, my lord Bishop, there only remains to send it.

BISHOP VIELLE: Except that you will not send it. Do not interrupt me, Mr. Deputy; it seems to me that I know you better than you might think. I've been following you for years; I've read all your speeches, and I believe I've grasped the meaning better, much better, than those to whom these speeches were addressed. You not only inspire in me that esteem, which is impossible not to accord to your intelligence and to your character; no, I know that there is in you more than a skillful orator, and more even than what is called (with a smile) a good citizen; there is in you ... a soul, and one that will not allow you to send this letter.

MOIRANS: And if it was this very soul that ordered me to send it?

BISHOP VIELLE: This hypothesis, I regret to say, does not bear up to examination; for your soul is that of a son of the Church.

MOIRANS: Can you be sure, Bishop?

BISHOP VIELLE: Absolutely sure, Mr. Deputy; and I warn you even that it would be futile to try to make me doubt it, because your life would rise up against your words and destroy them.

MOIRANS: My life, my lord Bishop, are you so sure then of knowing it well?

BISHOP VIELLE: Yes. Your actions are there.

MOIRANS: But can you know if my life, my real life, hasn't been else-where, rather that in my actions?

BISHOP VIELLE: I will not follow you into this distinction; outside of our acts, there is only room for the image we have of ourselves, and that image is not us. (*Moirans is going to interrupt him.*) Your life has been that of a militant Christian, it is for no one, not even you to deny it; for reasons over which it is not for me to insist and that I am not sure of penetrating entirely, it is possible that you might be interested in hiding it from your-self; but it is not in your power to destroy the past; at most you might think yourself capable of denying it; as to effectively deny it, that is another matter—and we shall see.

MOIRANS: My lord Bishop, it is impossible for me to understand you; suppose for a moment that while pursuing what you wish to call the life of a Christian activist, I entertained thoughts that were not really those of a Christian, that my actions did not accurately reflect these thoughts ...

BISHOP VIELLE: What were these actions otherwise thoughts, but expressed words after all? Would you like to make me believe that these words were misleading, that they were intended to mislead your audience about your true ideas? It must be a powerful interest which urges you to alter your past in your own eyes, so much so that you seek to overload it with such serious suspicion. I have no doubt, take note, of your sincerity now, nor for that matter of that in the past; but I warn you against the interpretations that your words will not fail to suggest to a speaker less favorably disposed that I am in your regard, and less informed about your situation.

MOIRANS: And yet, my lord Bishop, when you were saying just now that you thought to have better fathomed than many of my listeners the meaning of my words ...

BISHOP VIELLE: I wanted to say that behind the literalness of expressions which you used, I often thought to discern a more profound meaning, and one more spiritual.

MOIRANS: Well then, my lord Bishop, if my present words are explained according to you, as the desire to distort my past, this very desire, to what do you attribute it?

BISHOP VIELLE: I'm waiting for you to explain it honestly to me, I'm waiting for you reveal to me the reasons that have made you capable of considering for a moment to send this letter. They have already claimed that you were tired, overworked ... (*Moirans wants to interrupt.*) I do not believe in these reasons. A man like you cannot for an instant consider such a decision without serious reasons which cannot be physical. There is already a small problem which is from the past but which intrigues me, I must admit; and I would be very grateful to you, my dear Deputy, if you do me the favor of helping me to clarify it.

MOIRANS: (*bitterly*) How one feels you are sure of your power, my lord Bishop! And how one finds oneself fragile and inconsequential before you. You have for yourself the strength of twenty centuries ...

BISHOP VIELLE: What are you saying to me? This strength is in you, and I have only come here so that you might become aware of it; do you think me capable of pretending to influence your decisions in any way? No; if it had been necessary, I would have limited myself to call your attention to several points ... but I am happy to see that it is not necessary, for I know that you are not even dreaming any longer of sending this letter.

MOIRANS: Your triumph is premature, my lord Bishop. This letter will go out.

BISHOP VIELLE: There was the desire to defy me in that sentence, admit it; it leaves me unmoved as well. You are extending your arm to ring—you are going to give this letter to a servant: do you think you are demonstrating by that what you would call, I suppose, free thought? You would be wrong; because what you call an act would only be a gesture.

MOIRANS: My lord, you don't see that I am no longer capable, that it would only be a masquerade. I am no longer Catholic.

BISHOP VIELLE: For ten minutes I've been expecting that sentence. Do you think one can stop being a Catholic? One does not cease being a Catholic just as one never ceases being a creature. You think that Catholicism is like a color with which our thinking is tinted, and which can be erased by the influence of I don't know what reflections and I don't know what experiences (extending his hand), I do not wish to know them. But no. He is in us well beyond what we can attain, well beyond what we can change: what we can attain and change is so little! Cease to be Catholic! You remind me—pardon this anecdote—of a small child, who seeing himself maltreated by his classmates and noticing that they never hit his sister, said: "Papa, I don't want to be a little boy anymore." Your religion is in you, but it is not of you. Nothing stops that which is growing; and a Catholic …

MOIRANS: And if I have never been a Catholic? (*A silence.*)

BISHOP VIELLE: Allow me one question, my dear Deputy: If someone came six months ago to say to your face: "You are not Catholic," would you have answered: "It's true."

MOIRANS: Do you think to prove something? What if I deluded myself …

BISHOP VIELLE: It is not that you have deluded yourself. By the glow of your present concerns your past appears in a new light, so that you come to ask yourself if you have been Catholic (*he has a smile*), and to think that perhaps you have never been one—that is what I do not contest; but that you might think that I who know your past, that I will welcome such extravagant interpretations (excuse the term) that it pleases you to give, that is what makes me smile.

MOIRANS: My lord, how can I convince you?

BISHOP VIELLE: Under the present circumstances, that is impossible for you; you would come to make a profession of atheism and to assure me that you have never believed in the immortality of the soul; I would attribute these declarations to your present disordered state, and I would refuse to have them cast the slightest suspicion upon your past sincerity.

MOIRANS: But why? Why?

BISHOP VIELLE: (*bolstering his words*) The church doesn't know how to accept the services of an imposter; now you have been for her, no one can deny it, a good servant.

MOIRANS: So you don't want to believe that …

BISHOP VIELLE: I cannot believe it.

MOIRANS: But my lord Bishop, even if you are telling the truth, if it is as a result of my present anxieties that all my past appears in a false light, can I now silence my present scruples, forget my doubts?

BISHOP VIELLE: I'd like to see you prove me right because to hear you speak one might have said just now that your doubts were not of recent date and your scruples would have seemed tardy. I congratulate myself to only have seen in your words the expression of disarray, still incomprehensible to me, I admit it, yet it's where I find you immersed.

MOIRANS: Forgive me, my lord Bishop, but you do not grasp the problem … My thinking had built a castle, a castle of sand, I understand it now, but one where it seemed that it was able to live and subsist; I believed myself still Catholic—perhaps I was: I do not know. But this castle has crumbled; everywhere around me I note the dismal rubble; the shore is quite littered with it. I seemed to be sheltered from winds and tide, and here I am now level with the beach open to all hurricanes. Understand, my lord Bishop, this fortress of my faith that seemed impregnable, it has collapsed. It is myself now that it is a question of defending against the assault of all doubts—how could I even think of fighting disbelief when perhaps it is undermining me at this moment?

BISHOP VIELLE: Your words are an enigma for me. What is this sand-castle? As sings the heretic, "A Mighty Fortress is Our God." The house of God is vast; there is a place in it for all, even for you. What are these uncertainties that strike you? They cannot be doubts of an historical order; I esteem you too much, Mr. Deputy, to think you capable of letting yourself be shaken by what they call exegesis. (*He smiles.*)

MOIRANS: Thank you, my lord Bishop, for not thinking me at the mercy of such weak arguments. No. It's something else. My daughter … (*he is troubled*) perhaps you know it already; my youngest daughter is resolved to take the veil.

BISHOP VIELLE: What! That is the explanation!

MOIRANS: At that very thought, I can no longer conceal to you, my lord, beyond the mediocre dilemmas, where questions cease, I had built for myself a certainty. Finding in it and in these very assertions, the only beyond that could satisfy it, my thought lived in serenity. And now, here they are, the old questions that haunt me again! Do you possess a secret inaccessible to my thinking or on the contrary, this secret—is it not the old imagination that I thought I had killed? My lord Bishop, this question can only resolve itself within me and by me—but it would be necessary however, that it be resolved in God, independently of the mind, in some intelligible and foreign zone that the soul would reach after leaving the body. Here I begin to regret the time when the truth was for me a mysterious land toward which we sail and that one discovers one evening on the horizon—a land of hope and of magic in which is teeming unknown vegetation. Alas! It is hard that the truth is not discovered like that; but it is even harder that this certainty that I thought to have conquered now seems so precarious, that certainty that the truth is only the agile and harmonious dance of our reasoning ... if you could understand my lord Bishop, perhaps you would be able to heal; but no: your eyes are too assured, your smile is too undisturbed, you could not know the latest tribulations, you've kept well away from formidable reefs and the song of the Sirens has not even reached your ears ... I'm relapsing, you see, into this mediocre doubt of those for whom it is true or false ... to doubt God as one doubts an event, to doubt eternity as one doubts a news item. To say: "it's possible, but it's not proven, many deny it;" to relapse ... to relapse ... (*he makes a gesture of distress*). And I turn into myself again, crying after that lost Eden ... All this for this child who without a regret, without uncertainty, goes her way into the night. I have a vision of her life that will spend itself entirely in the service of God, and I think the sublime hopes on which she is hanging are only ...

BISHOP VIELLE: Don't say anymore my son, I have patiently listened to your confession. I think I now fathom your distress.

MOIRANS: Consider, my lord Bishop, this glorious world where fervor transports the believer escapes me.

BISHOP VIELLE: It suffices that you keep the nostalgia so that one might not say in truth that you have lost it. The fallen have no regrets, they do not know the disquiet which undermines you. The moment has come, my son, to take heart. Only your present pain matters; the past, you are interpreting, you are looking at it through your present doubts; you yourself no longer know what you have believed. (*Moirans wants to interrupt him.*) I don't want to remember the imprudent words that have escaped you, for these words were lying.

MOIRANS: And yet, my lord Bishop ...

BISHOP VIELLE: You must defer the examination of conscience to which your scruples prompt you; believe me my son, the disposition in which I find you removes all value from the conclusions you would draw. Only your present anxieties merit taking into account. Rest assured. I understand your emotion and perhaps even God cannot see it without being touched; that on the eve of this great separation, prelude to a holy union that the mind cannot even conceive, your paternal tenderness is anxious and doubts, yes, doubts—who then would impute to you a crime? I am able to tell you now: just a little while ago the affection that I have for you was troubled; I feared many other errors. But no: before this great mystery of Grace that has touched your child, you only fear what many fathers have felt before you. Do not interrupt me my son, for I bring you the assurance which your heart needs. Today more than yesterday the path that you must follow is drawn. Whether you like it or not, you are a man of action, and it is only in action that you will find a remedy to the anxiety that devours you. It is not by falling back on yourself that you will recover, because doubt is spread and deepened under the constant gaze of one who considers it: it is by fighting for this faith which, I affirm to you, my son, has remained yours and which you will soon renew, perhaps tomorrow, after you have resisted the temptation to think you've been abandoned!

MOIRANS: Perhaps you are right, my lord Bishop, yes, perhaps I will recover it after the struggle. Perhaps earlier I went astray by doubting even my past fervor; perhaps I have affirmed rightly long ago that in spite of appearances, and some resistance that my reason might oppose to the images and the metaphors that wrap around the great religious thoughts for common men, it is only one way of believing. And yet, my lord Bishop, when the prestige of your presence and of your words will be dispelled ...

BISHOP VIELLE: I am repeating to you my son, there is nothing said here that is not in you and is not coming from you. You have regained the mastery of yourself; it behooves you to keep it. (*He rises.*)

MOIRANS: Allow me, my lord Bishop, to accompany you. (*They go out together.*)

Act Three: Scene Four

Mrs. Moirans, Father Grandin, then Moirans

FATHER GRANDIN: (*coming in with Mrs. Moirans*) Be assured, madam, that all danger is now removed. No one can resist the eloquence of the Bishop.

MRS. MOIRANS: God grant that what you say is true, Reverend Father ... , but if the letter has already gone out!

FATHER GRANDIN: It would still not be an irreparable misfortune; Mr. Moirans would retain the possibility of changing his decision ...

MOIRANS: (*coming in*) I cannot say anything; I am exhausted. Reverend Father, make sure that they leave me alone for a while.

MRS. MOIRANS: But that letter, Roger ...

MOIRANS: I myself still don't know if I will mail it.

CLARISSE: Father, you must send it.

MRS. MOIRANS: Clarisse!

FATHER GRANDIN: Be careful, my child. In these circumstances you must ...

CLARISSE: Reverend Father, I am the only one here who can understand. Father!

MRS. MOIRANS: Your father is very tired.

REVEREND FATHER: My child ...

CLARISSE: He must listen to me.

MRS. MOIRANS: Roger, you wish? ... (*Moirans nods "yes"; they go out.*)

Act Three: Scene Five

Clarisse, Moirans

CLARISSE: (*ardently*) Father, I see that you hesitate ... I don't know what the Bishop could tell you ... but I am sure that this letter must go out; I am sure that you must renounce this life, because it is the life of a lie. If there is the hope that you go back to the simplicity of soul and truth, it is on condition that you retire from these struggles in which one loses the consciousness of what one is and what one believes. Father, I reflected a lot last night, and now I think I understand what your life must have been; I don't judge it, you see, I do not have the right to, but I know that you are tired of those proud and solitary games in which your thinking has indulged for a long time. Yesterday, you spoke of the faith of the humble and you said that you despise it, but you know yourself that it is the greatest good, it is the only good; if there is a path that can bring you to this lost paradise, I say it is that one. I understood yesterday that something was falling apart, and I read in your eyes a huge disappointment; but it is that which still allows for hope. Erase within yourself the memory of those vain years; forget those reckless efforts, those ungodly efforts; renounce your former life, father, humble yourself before the true faith.

MOIRANS: This faith has perhaps never ceased to be mine; and there was in my anguish of yesterday only the pain of a father who sees his child bury herself alive.

CLARISSE: In your words of yesterday I felt the winds of negation.

MOIRANS: Those words which frightened you were no doubt the cry of my heartfelt distress.

CLARISSE: Who has come then to pour into your soul, clairvoyant at last, torn apart at last, this reassuring and dangerous illusion? Father, I read into your soul yesterday and that soul is one of an unbeliever.

MOIRANS: What do you know of me?

CLARISSE: I am guessing it's my lord Bishop who came to lull your anguish with those misleading words, it was he who sought to persuade you that you have never ceased to be a Catholic. Father, one cannot believe in the abstract, one cannot believe in a vacuum. And it seems to me now that you were only looking for the religion of beautiful attitudes of soul and stirring thoughts.

MOIRANS: (harshly) You seem to delight in reopening my wound. Even if you would be right, even if what you call true faith would have been foreign to me ... what good is it now? Wouldn't it be better if I were able to persuade myself of the contrary? Wouldn't it be better if this beneficent illusion remained in me? The Bishop spoke wisely, humanely, and you, you arm yourself with that sword too heavy for your child hands.

CLARISSE: So you would have agreed to lose yourself?

MOIRANS: Just now as he enveloped me in his obscure sentences, I was drinking in his words and with them peace entered me. Now peace is all that I need, you understand, peace at any price, and now you must come to destroy it in me, the peace that I found again at last ... You are cruel, Clarisse, like all those people that one has loved too much. I feel now the old anguish returning to me, now I understand again why I wrote that letter. I ... Ah! Why, and what have I done to you? Who gave you the right to torture me like this?

CLARISSE: He who has said: "I am the Truth and the Life."

MOIRANS: So you think yourself his interpreter! You think he has charged you to plunge me again into this night of uncertainty from which I have slowly raised myself by faith? You are only a presumptuous and cruel child and if I was able I would laugh at your infatuation. (*With another tone.*) Clarisse, I had overcome doubts, I had even overcome interrogations; my thought was freed from the jail in which mediocre souls debated. Above them, well above, I was floating. You spoke just now of a paradise lost, the paradise I am crying over is not the one that you are speaking of; it is one of liberated beliefs that are no longer held bound to earth by the constant fear of the intention. And it is you who have caused this enchanted world to vanish, where my soul at last possessed itself; it is you who renew all my old anxieties by your foolish project. Again my thoughts hypnotize themselves on a beyond where prayers can be productive; again my fantasy invents, just as when I was a child, mysterious worlds in which the dead are reborn. I read it in your eyes, the sense of my words escapes you; you will never know that glorious liberty which was mine. I see well now that they were misleading, the similarities that I thought to discover yesterday, between our two souls; you are meant to serve. Bow down before the master in whom you believe; you are not worthy to know that the principle of his power is in the act by which you adore him. Farewell. (*He is going to go out.*)

CLARISSE: (*in a trembling voice*) The veil of ambiguity is torn, this time you have spoken your thoughts, and you have considered carefully... Pardon, but I cannot regret anything ... It had to be ... Perhaps these are the last words that we will exchange. Tell me that this letter will go out. (*A long silence.*)

MOIRANS: (*in a changed voice*) That only depends on a single being, and that being is you.

CLARISSE: (*frightened*) What do you mean?

MOIRANS: If you renounce entering the convent, this letter will go out. If not ... (*He makes a move to tear up the letter.*)

CLARISSE: But for what reason? Why?

MOIRANS: If you inflict on me the deadly pain of seeing you bury yourself in the oblivion of the cloister, there will only be salvation for me in action; as my lord Bishop said just a short while ago, only action heals—perhaps. I will only be able to give up this existence that has become necessary to me if you stay; we will leave together, we will travel ...

CLARISSE: (*with anguish*) Father, you are not speaking seriously. The problem for you can only be debated between yourself and ... (*she stops*). It is for your conscience to decide. You do not have to take care of me. Everything has to occur between you and your conscience.

MOIRANS: They are words. You are free to place the question on ideal ground where entities act on each other. In fact ... I am growing old, you understand, and I need someone or something that might keep me holding on to life. You can play this role, Clarisse, you alone can do it. If you refuse, I shall be obliged to tear up this letter. Oh! I know you would willingly propose to me other, more harmless distractions: visits to the poor of the parish, or edifying discussions with the parish priest, or even taking notes from pious readings which would bring me back to the right path. You see, I am guessing the charming proposals that you would not hesitate to make, if I were to let you speak. Unfortunately, it is not about that; I find myself poorly disposed to take on the role of good-natured old man. There are only two alternatives, and they are the ones that I have said.

CLARISSE: Father, the role you are playing is atrocious. You are trying to exploit the outrage that I feel at the thought of that life of lies with which you refuse to break, you seek to exploit the yearning that I would have had (*Moirans smiles*) to work for your salvation; don't smile, it's really a question of salvation right now. How far down do you have to descend in order to threaten this monstrous blackmail? (*A silence*) But it is useless, my duty cannot be to give in; I sense that it would be cowardice to accept this bargain; it's not possible that the call that I heard has been in vain and that I must now ... (*wringing her hands*.) My God, enlighten me, give me a sign ...

MOIRANS: You must have signs now! You become demanding ...

CLARISSE: Besides ... My sacrifice would not save you; what would be the value of your renunciation if it was bought?

MOIRANS: (*with profound irony*) I thought that prayers for the salvation of others were answered; a sacrifice, is it less efficacious?

CLARISSE: Do not profane these mysteries.

MOIRANS: It is true that it is easier to pray—especially when one only has that to do.

CLARISSE: (*desperate*) I cannot, I must not.

MOIRANS: "I cannot" is enough. That's good, I know now where I stand on the spirit with which you approach your new life. It's not the danger that attracts you, as you were saying yesterday; no, what beckons to you is the moral comfort of a peaceful life in which through some regulated dose of fervor, and some small sacrifices, one is assured of gaining one's salvation. Go. Prepare yourself wisely for blessedness as one prepares for a contest. Above all, not too much zeal; that is paid in the aftermath. Moderation. Reasonable health; and small innocent distractions from time to time.

CLARISSE: (*holding her ears*) I do not want to hear it.

Act Three: Scene Six

The same characters; Mrs. Moirans

MRS. MOIRANS: What's happening? You look thoroughly upset.

CLARISSE: Mama, I want to leave right away. I want to go there immediately.

MRS. MOIRANS: Look, you're not reasonable, it would be impulsive; and then it's impossible.

CLARISSE: I cannot stay here.

MRS. MOIRANS: But you are crazy. (*During this time Moirans has taken the letter and torn it up.*) Roger! You have torn up the letter?

MOIRANS: Yes.

MRS. MOIRANS: Clarisse! You should be happy. Your father …

CLARISSE: Mama, I beg you, let me leave tonight. You must.

MRS. MOIRANS: We'll ask Reverend Father what he thinks about it; he has just had a conversation with your sister.

CLARISSE: Is he still here?

MRS. MOIRANS: You'd like to speak to him?

CLARISSE: Yes.

MRS. MOIRANS: (*calling*) Reverend Father, can you come here a moment?

MOIRANS: Ah!, but he spends his life here!

MRS. MOIRANS: (*to Father who enters*) Clarisse would like to speak with you.

MOIRANS: (*to his daughter*) That's it, go seek a little comfort from Reverend Father; he has plenty to spare. (He goes out.)

MRS. MOIRANS: My God, what is happening? (*Father gives her a sign to leave him alone with Clarisse; she goes out.*)

Act Three: Scene Seven

Clarisse, Reverend Father Grandin

FATHER GRANDIN: (with kindness) What is it my child?

CLARISSE: Reverend Father, I am in the worst anxiety … and what is most awful, it's that I cannot even explain everything to you … I can only ask you a question for which it's necessary that you perceive … My whole life depends on it.

FATHER GRANDIN: Then what is this question?

CLARISSE: Can the vocation to the cloister be a temptation? Tell me, can it? Or is it surely fool-proof, and when one has heard … the call, can one go there without any hesitation, without scruple, plugging one's ears so as not to hear the voices that would hold you back?

FATHER GRANDIN: First of all, calm down, my child; I see you are all upset, overexcited.

CLARISSE: Tell me, Reverend Father!

FATHER GRANDIN: Promise me to remain calm.

CLARISSE: I promise you … but this question?

FATHER GRANDIN: This question is resolved very easily. No doubt it can happen that one thinks to hear the call that you speak of without really having a religious vocation. I remember that in the big Seminary …

CLARISSE: It's not that, Reverend Father.

FATHER GRANDIN: You must be careful then; but consider my child, that it's not a question of pronouncing your vows yet. You will have a lot of time to seek counsel, to interrogate yourself; and even ...

CLARISSE: The question is different.

FATHER GRANDIN: Come, my child, don't interrupt me every minute. If you feel that the life of the world attracts you, that you cannot live far from it, if doubts come about the sustainability of your vocation, your duty—I say your duty—will be to take account of it; because God wants us to serve voluntarily. What is it? Why are you looking at me like that? I no longer know what I was going to say.

CLARISSE: Pardon me, Reverend Father, but you don't see what my doubt is. I am not afraid that something is smothering this vocation in me; I know that my most ardent desire is to consecrate my life to the service of God. I will not be one of those who, after hours of enthusiasm and fervor, return slowly to the life they have left, to fix on it a look full of tears.

FATHER GRANDIN: Those are imprudent words, my child; no one can respond for himself; your zeal pleases me however, and ...

CLARISSE: I can answer for myself; but what I wonder is if my real duty wouldn't be to conquer within myself this desire for the cloister, to conquer this irresistible appeal that leads me to be a religious ...

FATHER GRANDIN: (*opening his eyes wide*) And why should you, my daughter?

CLARISSE: If as he said just a short while ago, that it was the great peace of the convent which attracted me? If what I thought to be a victory was only an escape? Reverend Father, perhaps life makes me afraid; perhaps I am too cowardly to live like other people. Perhaps a horrible illusion, due to my own weakness, has made me see as the most glorious existence what is only the easiest existence.

FATHER GRANDIN: The easiest! Do you think that, my child? It is not at all an easy life that awaits you, and I fear for your disappointments. When you will have to rise in the middle of the night ...

CLARISSE: *(fearfully)* Is this what you recognize as a difficult life?

FATHER GRANDIN: You will have to break with many pleasurable habits, and I will say, comfort ...

CLARISSE: *(controlling herself)* Understand me, Reverend Father, all of that does not frighten me at all. It is not a question of those sacrifices.

FATHER GRANDIN: Perhaps they will seem heavier to you than you might think.

CLARISSE: It's a question of dangers ... spiritual ones; if it was the certainty of a shelter against the great perils of thought!

FATHER GRANDIN: For once, I do not understand you.

CLARISSE: The worry over my salvation ... if it risked becoming for me there the exclusive preoccupation?

FATHER GRANDIN: I wouldn't see that as such a big misfortune. We are all here in order to work for our salvation, the best we can.

CLARISSE: Reverend Father, I feel that you are miles away from understanding me.

FATHER GRANDIN: Indeed, I am afraid of not clearly understanding what is tormenting you. I perceive however ... but these worries will melt away, you'll see. *(He wants to get up.)*

CLARISSE: It's now, Reverend Father, it is right now that an answer is necessary for my anguish.

FATHER GRANDIN: You will see, while you are there, leading that holy existence, all will seem much simpler ...

CLARISSE: But isn't that the worst danger? If little by little, as he said (*lowering her voice*), we become stupid!

FATHER GRANDIN: (*who hasn't heard*) What did you say?

CLARISSE: If little by little one forgets that the gate of heaven is a narrow gate, if one's mind is dulled by easy certainties and ... (*with fright*) Father, father, if you heard me, you would be happy! (*Covering her face with her hands.*) I no longer know, I no longer know.

FATHER GRANDIN: It's a little excitement, very natural on the eve of making such a serious resolution. I will go to see you, my child, and we will talk about these issues which worry you.. Oh! I do not deny it. You must not be so terribly afraid. Unfortunately I cannot remain any longer right now. But I will go to see you, the priest is a like the doctor of the soul. You will entrust your thoughts to me.

CLARISSE: (*disgusted*) I ...

FATHER GRANDIN: I hope to ease your mind. Your concerns are pleasing to God. Besides, I read on your face that already you see more clearly into yourself.

CLARISSE: Yes, it's true.

FATHER GRANDIN: I told you so. And as to your original question, I think you now understand that it wasn't possible for me to take it seriously.

CLARISSE: Yes ...

FATHER GRANDIN: How would it be a temptation ...

CLARISSE: (*in an ambiguous tone of voice*) To seek the most safe way of resisting all temptation?

FATHER GRANDIN: (*rising*) That's it, that's it. Oh no, my rheumatism! It's nothing, don't accompany me, my daughter, I know the way. (*He goes out.*)

CLARISSE: (*alone, running to the door*) Father, father, be happy: I am staying with you.

CURTAIN

ACT FOUR

(One year later. A sitting room in a villa alongside a lake in Italy.)

Act Four: Scene One

Clarisse, Moirans

MOIRANS: Your mother and Theresa have not yet come down?

CLARISSE: The trip has tired them, and they said last night that they were getting up late.

MOIRANS: I find both of them changed. Your mother has aged.

CLARISSE: It's true.

MOIRANS: And I have the impression that your sister wears make-up.

CLARISSE: It's possible. *(A silence.)*

MOIRANS: There it goes. Our nice little life together interrupted, if not *(He has an expressive gesture)* ... the best things do not last, unfortunately! But there were good times. Do you remember our evenings on the Pincio, and certain afternoons ...

CLARISSE: I want to carry these memories within me without counting them. We feel rich only when we don't count our joys.

MOIRANS: You don't have your usual air about you today; one would say you didn't sleep well.

CLARISSE: I didn't sleep well.

MOIRANS: Worries? *(Clarisse makes an evasive gesture.)* My little one, are you withdrawing your trust in me? It has been so good, this fraternal life. You don't know how precious it has been for me to be able to speak freely, to be able to talk about myself to you.

CLARISSE: I sometimes wonder if we don't create ourselves when we think we are talking about ourselves.

MOIRANS: You know me now, such as I am.

CLARISSE: Perhaps we are nothings. (*A silence.*)

MOIRANS: You are singular this morning. Do you agree that you're hiding something from me?

CLARISSE: It's not what little girls call a secret. Don't worry. I myself don't know exactly what it is. I think that distress is coming.

MOIRANS: Is it because of the arrival of your mother and your sister? ... Or rather is it because of Peter?

CLARISSE: The reasons come afterward.

MOIRANS: You mean that we only know them afterward.

CLARISSE: They only exist when we know them. (*A silence.*)

MOIRANS: What is this dry wisdom that I did not suspect in you?

CLARISSE: I would not know how to translate it into formulas.

MOIRANS: Admit that Peter is not a stranger to this unusual sadness. He is going to come very soon; he will ask me once more; what answer shall I give?

CLARISSE: I don't know.

MOIRANS: You don't permit me to let him have any hope? He loves you, Clarisse, and he is a loyal young man, I'm answering for him.

CLARISSE: Can you believe that that is enough?

MOIRANS: And yet I would have thought again ... now that all this is past ...

CLARISSE: How do you know that it is past?

MOIRANS: Why is it that today I sense you to be so tense and so secretive?

CLARISSE: You mustn't be angry with me, father.

MOIRANS: You do not love him, you don't think yourself able to love him?

CLARISSE: The problem is another.

MOIRANS: What is it? (*She doesn't answer.*) My poor child, you must create a simpler soul.

CLARISSE: Reverend Father told me the same thing, the last time that we chatted together.

MOIRANS: You know very well that he wasn't saying it in the same sense.

CLARISSE: You are mistaken, father; his purpose wasn't yours, but he thought and he spoke like you ... and what does the purpose matter? There is only the way of thinking that counts, or of not thinking. A more simple soul? So can we cripple ourselves, and should we? If it were suicide!

MOIRANS: Understand me, my child, on the contrary what I want is for you to live. The great complexities of thought kill life in us. There are diseases of the intelligence ... I tell you from experience; I am still very close to this painful past, and yet already I begin to judge it.

CLARISSE: Are you quite certain that it's health that you have recovered now? Remember how you would have judged, a year ago, your words of today, if you had been able to hear them.

MOIRANS: It is now that I see things in their proper light.

CLARISSE: There is no light that is more true than another. (*A silence.*)

MOIRANS: Peter is going to leave at the end of the week. Will he take away a certainty?

CLARISSE: His departure will not change my future.

MOIRANS: Your mother and your sister are here, I'll leave you with them. (*He goes out.*)

Act Four: Scene Two

Clarisse, Theresa, Mrs. Moirans

CLARISSE: Have you slept well?

MRS. MOIRANS: The beds are a little hard.

CLARISSE: They have brought you breakfast?

THERESA: They don't know how to make hot chocolate here.

MRS. MOIRANS: And this crystallized sugar does not melt. (*Looking around her.*) How long did your father rent it for?

CLARISSE: Until the summer. Count Favelli, to whom the villa belongs, arrives every year at the beginning of July.

THERESA: You didn't have to bother, both of you.

MRS. MOIRANS: And during that time … you will never know what I have been through.

CLARISSE: *(to her sister)* Have you finished with all the formalities?

THERESA: Thank God!

MRS. MOIRANS: Every day some insults. Some friends who no longer greet us.

CLARISSE: My poor mama!

MRS. MOIRANS: Your brother who set out to marry a dancer.

THERESA: The business of enraging papa.

MRS. MOIRANS: But this existence cannot last. What are we going to do?

CLARISSE: We don't know yet.

THERESA: *(in a whisper, designating her mother)* Her temperament has changed a lot.

MRS. MOIRANS: What is it you were saying?

THERESA: I am going for a walk in the garden; it looks quite lovely to me.

CLARISSE: Do you want me to go with you?

MRS. MOIRANS: *(to Clarisse)* Stay a moment, will you? *(Theresa goes out.)*

Act Four: Scene Three

Clarisse, Mrs. Moirans

MRS. MOIRANS: Now that Theresa has left, I can tell you that we have decided to not live together any more. Since the divorce your sister has taken a way of life that is impossible for me to get used to. She has extravagant outfits, she flaunts herself with people … and … (*She stops*).

CLARISSE: What mama?

MRS. MOIRANS: I'm afraid there is worse. There comes to the house a type of suave writer …

CLARISSE: Do you think he wants to marry her?

MRS. MOIRANS: He is married. (*A silence*) Clarisse, I am an unhappy woman, and if it wasn't for religion, I would have ceased living long ago … can we go to confession here?

CLARISSE: (*holding back a smile*) Obviously.

MRS. MOIRANS: What is the parish priest like?

CLARISSE: I don't know, I have never seen him.

MRS. MOIRANS: Ah … Tell me then, that former plan, is it absolutely ended? (*Clarisse does not respond.*) Go on, it's better that way. I would be disconsolate to see you cloistered … Do you know that you have really changed? I find you younger looking … and at the same time more of a woman.

CLARISSE: Ah!

MRS. MOIRANS: For a girl, you see, the best is still to marry … it's true that the examples that you have around you are hardly encouraging … but there are others. (*A short silence.*) Is Dr. Servan here?

CLARISSE: Yes.

MRS. MOIRANS: He met you by chance?

CLARISSE: No.

MRS. MOIRANS: Your father had written him that you were here?

CLARISSE: I think that he had written him to come join us.

MRS. MOIRANS: So then? ... Be careful. This is a man who believes in nothing. I well know; religion is perhaps less necessary for men than for women. But all the same, me, I would not trust ... a lad who did not even make his first communion; no use talking; there will always be something about that which will make people talk. This is not the man you need. But there are other issues. Me, for example? It's not in my interest to advise you to marry. What will become of me? I don't suppose that your father intends ...

CLARISSE: You should no longer live together.

MRS. MOIRANS: Besides, they would forbid me to do anything like that. (*Clarisse looks at her.*) Yes, it seems that your father wrote a letter to the Bishop in which he renounced all of his past ... but then, you know what my life will be all alone! I don't even have any longer poor Miss Amelia ... ah! If it wasn't for religion! ... All the same, if someone would have told me thirty years ago, that it would end like this ... it's hard. (*She makes the grimace of an old woman.*)

CLARISSE: And yet there are worse miseries than yours, there are more profound losses than yours.

MRS. MOIRANS: (*suddenly*) So you are not happy? He could not even make you happy? Ah! Yes, it's true!... Why did you follow him?

CLARISSE: Mama, you know that in leaving with him, it's not happiness that I was looking for.

MRS. MOIRANS: What were you looking for then?

CLARISSE: It matters little since I didn't find it.

MRS. MOIRANS: In spite of what you will say: if you suffer, it is only with your mind, and I …

CLARISSE: Do not be mistaken, Mother, one never suffers but with all one's soul.

Act Four: Scene Four

The same characters, Moirans

MOIRANS: (*entering*) I just saw Servan on the road; he will be here in about five minutes. You must know by now if he might have hope. You don't have the right to leave him in uncertainty any longer. He knows that you are aware of his feelings for you. You cannot speculate any longer about the shyness which prevents him from declaring himself openly. If necessary, you must get him to open up, and you must reveal to him your true intentions.

CLARISSE: If I don't know them myself?

MOIRANS: You must know them. Everything depends on you.

CLARISSE: This is precisely what is terrible.

MRS. MOIRANS: It seems to me, Roger, that it would be better …

MOIRANS: These delays can be of no use. Here he is.

Act Four: Scene Five

The same characters; Peter

PETER: Hello, madam. You have had a good trip?

MRS. MOIRANS: Thank you.

MOIRANS: Listen, my friend, we'll leave you with my daughter. We know perfectly well why you are here. It is useless to put on an act. I authorize and even invite you to tell Clarisse ... besides, she already knows. (*He leaves with his wife.*)

Act Four: Scene Six

Peter, Clarisse

CLARISSE: My father is right, it is useless to pretend further. I know you came to ask for my hand and that his consent is granted to you.

PETER: It's true ... but it's not like this that I would have wished ...

CLARISSE: Don't regret the many attempts at poor or conventional introductions. It wasn't necessary that there be anything like that between us.

PETER: And yet, now, even before you might have said anything, I sense that all is lost.

CLARISSE: Why?

PETER: Because you wouldn't have spoken like that if ... if you loved me. You do not love me.

CLARISSE: It's true, and yet I know that if I were to become your wife ...

PETER: What good is it? I am not a child who needs to be consoled.

CLARISSE: You don't understand me; I know that in refusing your offer, it is happiness that I reject ...

PETER: Pardon me; I do not believe you. Happiness is not something that you can reject like that.

CLARISSE: (*looking at him profoundly*) You think so?

PETER: I am sure of it.

CLARISSE: (*with bitterness*) And yet, it's because you would bring me happiness that I cannot accept. (*Controlling herself*) Listen: there are beings who are not born for happiness and who even if they were ever to have their share of it, would not know how to live with it. Pity them, even if their trepidation remains foreign to you.

PETER: Man cannot aspire to anything that is beyond happiness; this same trepidation is only the obsession of a vaguely imagined happiness, and that life cannot offer.

CLARISSE: You think so? (*A silence.*)

PETER: Farewell. I am more informed now; although ... (*He makes a gesture of weariness.*)

CLARISSE: Stay.

PETER: What's the point?

CLARISSE: You have the right to clearly know me; the love that I read in your eyes makes you worthy of this sad privilege. (*A silence.*) You must believe me my friend; I would not pardon you for making me happy. That may seem awful to you, but it is so. The life that you offer me ... ah! You cannot know how much I see all of its sweetness! (*Her eyes fill up with tears.*) To be a wife, to be a mother! Could you doubt what this vision is for me!

PETER: But it is only for you to ...

CLARISSE: No, no, in accepting your offer, I would cease to be me. Once before already ... think that if I had not placed before me the terrible word: temptation, I would be over there in the gray house where one prays day and night.

PETER: But this time, don't you see then that it is not temptation, that it is the call of nature and of life!

CLARISSE: The infallible instinct! Perhaps you are deifying it; to me it is only what survives in me from the beast.

PETER: Do not speak evil of the beasts; they are ignorant of the sufferings of pride and unnecessary stress.

CLARISSE: That is why they do not exist. To give up this time, it would be to deny all the past, it would be to recognize that by believing to resist temptation, I was perhaps obeying only a secret instinct, to I know not what well hidden deep within myself, and which by duping my pride would lead me to a detested end. This cannot be.

PETER: And yet if it's true?

CLARISSE: It's up to me that it be false.

PETER: Beware: that pride can lead to lying.

CLARISSE: There is no truth beyond my actions and the consciousness that I have of them. I am what I want to be, and I shatter by shaking the circle in which your reason locks me.

PETER: The obstinacy that you put into denying this truth, demonstrates it more than any argument. By believing that you free yourself, you remain a slave more than ever. It's still a slavery, the will to be free at any price. Pardon me, but I cannot resign myself to lose you for a chimera.

CLARISSE: Consider that what you call a chimera is still the only tie that still binds me to life. If I lost this faith in my freedom that you vainly seek to destroy, do not expect that it would be to follow you, my friend; there is some mourning from which a soul does not survive.

PETER: And yet ... there is another wisdom than yours, believe me; perhaps it does not fly above the clouds but at least it's not detached from life; perhaps it's only a lesser evil, at least it doesn't mutilate those who give themselves to it.

CLARISSE: A demanding consciousness is not satisfied with second best and I challenge any accommodating wisdom.

PETER: You practice the virtues of the catechism strangely; I thought your religion prescribed humility.

CLARISSE: (*painfully*) Religion is beyond our miserable speech.

PETER: And yet it is what is largely responsible. If it were not to support within yourself the hope of an afterlife, you would not be seeking to destroy within yourself all the seeds of happiness, all the seeds of life. That's what is awful. (*His voice is choking.*) If you had seen a hundred times, like me, life wavering in the eyes of the dying, flickering like a poor flame that is about to go out, you would know that this life is the only one and that it is precious; but no, you go like a hypnotized one toward those illusions ... (*With a bitter laugh.*) It's true that you will not know. The dead do not repent ... Let me tell you all my thoughts, since we will not see each other again. I do not even have the resource within me to admire you, because it is rough, for sure, the path to which you are committed; the door is narrow, but it opens to heaven.

CLARISSE: What do you know of heaven? What do you know of salvation? These are for you only words or images. But the kingdom of heaven is within us. It is not a land of miracle promised in the aftermath of death, it is the place of blessing which feeds faith inexhaustibly. Eternal life is not a hope, it is not a future, it is today.

PETER: How is it that your look grows sad as you speak? And why in the depths of your eyes did I see a dawning nostalgia?

CLARISSE: (*after a silence*) Farewell my friend. You were right. Words are useless.

PETER: That's it? ...

CLARISSE: Go now, I implore you not to insist.

PETER: Farewell. (*He leaves.*)

Act Four: Scene Seven

Clarisse, then Mrs. Moirans, then Moirans

MRS. MOIRANS: (*entering*) And so?

CLARISSE: (*still overwhelmed*) He left.

MOIRANS: (*entering*) Well?

CLARISSE: Father, I must speak to you. Pardon, mama ... in a little while ... surely ...

MRS. MOIRANS: That's it; always him! (*She goes out.*)

Act Four: Scene Eight

Clarisse, Moirans

MOIRANS: You didn't refuse?

CLARISSE: Father, listen to me ...

MOIRANS: You let him go?

CLARISSE: Father, have pity on me and do not insist. Let it no longer be a question of him. Go on, the worst is done, when one has had the courage to suffer like that ... the rest is easy. Do not look at me like that, your surprise cannot be sincere. (*With bitterness.*) Don't you remember those phrases that once excited your joy? I said that a life that is not dangerous is not worth living and I grew enthusiastic at the thought of the great winds on the summits. (*With increasing harshness.*) Those words. It's your presence that tore them from me, and it is only since then that they became my thoughts. Father, do you see that your responsibility is tremendous, because now I'm a wreck, and it's your fault.

MOIRANS: You see, you are unreasonable. I have had no influence in your decisions; only that you perhaps may have inherited my temper ...

CLARISSE: No, no, do not reject a mysterious fatality which has been the consequence of your actions. I see it all so clearly and I can no longer undo anything, nothing! (*She remains silent a moment.*) It is you who made me doubt and in doubting I became another. It is you who have sown in me this fatal thought that danger is worth it in and of itself. Consider ... I believed, I believed with the faith of the humble, that faith that you despise. (*Moirans makes a gesture.*) Yes, yes, you yourself have said it. I felt heaven so close, a sign, nothing but a sign and it would open (*She passes her hands over her forehead.*) It was more than a truth, it was the Being himself who was giving himself to me.

MOIRANS: My poor child, have I done anything to you to remove this precious faith? And didn't you yourself say that without me, perhaps you would not have had it?

CLARISSE: Do not awaken the other past; it is asleep. (*She thinks for a moment.*) You, the first one, the only one, you forced me to interpret my faith, and to think ... by a maleficent suggestion that I only now perceive, you have given rise in my soul to the idea that beyond my faith there was in me another thought, another desire, that made it right ... call it what you like. And the ... this thought took hold of me, it became all-powerful. The spirit of pride was my master. This is your crime, father. In wanting to explain my faith ... you killed it.

MOIRANS: It's not possible … if your belief is dead and I still refuse to admit it, it has occurred naturally like so many others, only later and more tragically.

CLARISSE: Never does faith die a natural death; in the order of ideas there are only suicides and murders.

MOIRANS: It's only a beautiful phrase, you see. The more I go, the more I understand how much it's folly to seek support outside of life in a mystical beyond, whether it be God or only freedom. The depth of things we do not know, we still do not know; all we know is that the same laws are at work in us and outside of us. Intellects go wrong like bodies, they grow old like bodies … If my life were to begin again, I would no longer seek to build it on the plan of the absolute. To build on the absolute, I know it now, is building on sand.

CLARISSE: (*fearfully*) Thus you have come to this miserable philosophy! (*Moirans makes a helpless gesture.*) Thus so much suffering has been spent in vain … Do not hope that I might follow you on the road of denial and betrayal.

MOIRANS: My poor Clarisse, I'm not asking you to follow me … perhaps later you will catch up to me … think, you've already come a long way. "An abyss separates us," … those were your words. Would you say them again today? Perhaps you are destined to come after me, and go through the same stages … It's not cheerful … but in the end I glimpse a kind of joy, oh! very humble …

CLARISSE: Whatever you might think, father, from today on our paths are separated forever.

MOIRANS: And yet, remember our winter in Italy … Clarisse, you will talk in vain; I felt reborn in you the taste for life. A new soul blossomed in you.

CLARISSE: And if I want to smother it? Understand me. Yes, it's true, I felt throbbing in me an unknown soul, a soul easy to please and who only wanted to live; like the former one, the proud one that you infused into me. But it will not be born. Earlier while Peter was speaking to me, it suddenly appeared to me: it was similar to a thousand others. Oh! The banality of its smile and its gestures! ... At the sight of it a great disgust came over me ... and it vanished without return. You are listening to me as if I were recounting a dream or a vision ... you still do not believe that all this is real, because that would risk darkening your life and prevent you from looking at landscapes. Evidently ... Perhaps I should leave you to your illusions, but no ... life has drawn us too close together for me to remain silent, it has tangled too much the threads of our destinies. I am just like you essentially, and this is why you understand me.

MOIRANS: (*fearfully*) But then what will become of you? The old dreams ...

CLARISSE: The old dreams are dead, alas! I cannot even regret the happiness from which you exiled me. It is too foreign to me. But you, father! Drop those veils which prevent you from seeing clearly, and for just one minute look at the disaster of which you are the cause ... You must show yourself the spectacle. You are too brave to flee the punishment.

MOIRANS: So be it, speak.

CLARISSE: If I were entering into religion now it would no longer be to live my faith, it would only be to escape. By serving a God in whom I no longer have faith, I would be profaning the religious fervor that I had for him; it is because his religion is still dear to me that I can no longer participate in it. Understand, father; I now know that intoxication of the summits that you invited me to share with you; I know what this abstract fervor is that rises into the void and that does not exalt the vision of any God. But that which delighted you is torture for me; on the summit where you were singing victory, I only feel vertigo; I am no longer free, I am exiled; I cry like a lost country what I now know to be only a chimerical world. It is between heaven and earth that the years will flow that separate me from death, too low to live in God, too high to live among men. They are to be pitied, those born for eternity and whom eternity did not want.

MOIRANS: What do you know about the future? I understand your pain, and in your words I felt pass the echo of my old torments. But you are young, so many things can happen ... and then, even though that should be ... I've searched in vain ... I would have only been the unconscious instrument in the hands of destiny. You must come back to that. Thoughts do not communicate.

CLARISSE: It's convenient for you to believe it, father, be careful—it is this illusion that has led you astray. It seemed in the past that you were only involving yourself; you wanted to ignore the mysterious beyond where our actions fall. Ideas are actions too ... and they work outside of us; slowly, painfully they break through, like an underground current that disintegrates the rocks.

MOIRANS: Thus it would be possible? Solitude itself would be an illusion and one would not even have the right to think his thoughts? I would have given to another this atrocious power to depend on me? (*He falls silent, afflicted.*)

CLARISSE: At last, father, you have understood me; yes, you have given me this terrible power.

MOIRANS: For the first time I feel like a slave ... you are there like the one who no longer has anything to expect and for whom everything is over.

CLARISSE: Only one road is still open.

MOIRANS: (*with a cry*) You want to kill yourself!

CLARISSE: (*with firmness*) No, father, I swear to you I will not kill myself. This very master whom you gave to me, forbade me. The road is harder, alas!

MOIRANS: My child, have pity. The curtain is torn; I do see now. (*A long silence.*)

CLARISSE: I know now that you have atoned.

MOIRANS: One would say that you're happy now.

CLARISSE: Yes, father, I think I'm happy: at the crossroads, before parting forever ... (*She stops.*)

MOIRANS: That cannot be. Whatever you may have resolved, I object to that ...

CLARISSE: Father, remember the power that you have given me.

MOIRANS: I cannot; I want to break these too strong attachments.

CLARISSE: In seeking to break them you would only be tightening them.

MOIRANS: It's necessary that you be able to forget.

CLARISSE: You will not destroy in me the will to remember. That will is mine.

MOIRANS: But you said so yourself, it is I who infused it in you. Why did I formerly feel this guilty need to have you close by? I recall my fever at the time. Why didn't I respect your faith and why did I want to understand it?

CLARISSE: Perhaps this fever back then was what in your life most resembled true love. Because at that time solitude weighed down on you; at that time you suffered.

MOIRANS: Why was it that you were the victim of this suffering?

CLARISSE: (*with a sad smile*) The sterile offering of a life was perhaps necessary to atone for your solitude; for you have lived alone among men.

MOIRANS: In what heaven does this mysterious justice reside?

CLARISSE: It suffices that the thought of order be in us so that we might affirm that it is.

MOIRANS: And yet, if no God has wanted it ...

CLARISSE: Father, remember: our thoughts must know how to be sufficient unto themselves. They do not emanate from any center, no original world is mirrored in their waters.

MOIRANS: I recognize now my wisdom of days gone by; why is it that it no longer has the same look?

CLARISSE: It's that it has gone through life.

Act Four: Scene Nine

The same characters; Mrs. Moirans

MRS. MOIRANS: I don't know what the matter is with Theresa. She is like a madwoman ...

CLARISSE: What has happened?

MRS. MOIRANS: It's a letter that the postman brought in just now; while she was reading, I saw her face contract, and she has just had a kind of nervous breakdown.

CLARISSE: What can that be all about?

MOIRANS: We are going to find out. Theresa! Theresa!

THERESA: (*offstage, one does not see her*) I'm packing.

MOIRANS: Why are you packing?

THERESA: Yes, I am leaving again.

MRS. MOIRANS: But you are mad. (*To the others.*) I am going to go to her.

MOIRANS: She is going to come here. (*Shouting*) Theresa, I am asking you to come down immediately. You hear me.

MRS. MOIRANS: My God, what is going to happen?

THERESA: (*appearing, red-eyed*) What do you want? The letter that I just received obliges me to return immediately.

MOIRANS: What is this letter?

MRS. MOIRANS: (*fearfully*) Would it be ...

THERESA: Yes, it is from Maurice. He wants to leave me. (*Moirans has a contemptuous smile.*)

MRS. MOIRANS: So you are admitting to — ... Is it possible? You had such good sense as a child! That's all we need. (*She is in tears.*)

THERESA: Mama, I'm not telling you anything new. It's not worth pretending.

MRS. MOIRANS: (*furious*) You dare to speak to me like that? All is over between us.

THERESA: It will be worse for you!

Act Four: Scene Ten

The same characters, less Theresa

MRS. MOIRANS: My God, what will become of me? Everyone wants my death ... besides, you will soon be happy. I feel that I am not long for this world. If it weren't for religion ... (*She collapses into an armchair sobbing.*)

CLARISSE: (*approaching her, softly*) Mama, listen.

MRS. MOIRANS: No, no, you too are hard! Oh, hard! I really saw it just now.

CLARISSE: (*the same*) Mama!

MRS. MOIRANS: You will soon be rid of me.

CLARISSE: Mama, do you hear me?

MOIRANS: What are you going to say to her?

CLARISSE: I am here, mama, here. (*She strokes the forehead.*)

MOIRANS: Clarisse, it's not possible.

MRS. MOIRANS: Leave me.

CLARISSE: Mama, calm yourself ... listen: I will not leave you. You hear me ... I will not leave you.

MRS. MOIRANS: (*in an indistinct voice*) You say that ...

CLARISSE: I say that because it will be so. You hear me, I will not leave you ever again.

MRS. MOIRANS: I don't even have a cook; Josephine has left.

CLARISSE: Really?

MRS. MOIRANS: Didn't I tell you? She asked for an increase, and as I refused, she got angry, she said some horrible things, I had to turn her out.

CLARISSE: We'll find someone else.

MRS. MOIRANS: You must not apply to an employment agency. (*During all this time MOIRANS has remained against the wall, his head in his hands.*) Perhaps through advertising ...

CLARISSE: We'll see.

MRS. MOIRANS: (*with irritation*) In employment agencies, the advertisements are always rewritten.

CLARISSE: We won't go there.

MOIRANS: (*in a low voice*) Stop this comedy; you cannot seriously think of living with this woman.

CLARISSE: (*to her mother*) Come now, mama; you are tired, you will rest well on the chaise-longue. We are going to find a newspaper where we can place an ad.

MRS. MOIRANS: I can very well go upstairs alone; I don't need anyone, thank God.

CLARISSE: You prefer to go upstairs alone?

MRS. MOIRANS: Yes, I do! (*She goes out.*)

Act Four: Scene Eleven

Moirans, Clarisse

MOIRANS: So then, that's it, the only road open?

CLARISSE: That is it.

MOIRANS: Well, I fear in effect that our paths will diverge.

CLARISSE: I told you so.

MOIRANS: So you can envisage without a shudder the thought of shutting yourself up with this..? You can do it? ...

CLARISSE: I can do it.

MOIRANS: (*passing his hands over his forehead*) It's mad, it's ...

CLARISSE: Father, don't start again. I am happy to see that your sadness of a little while ago has passed. We will not inconvenience you too much. That is all that matters.

MOIRANS: (*crying out*) My little one ... you are all that I have left.

CLARISSE: And for her? What is left for her?

MOIRANS: (*with contempt*) Her!

CLARISSE: I listened to you at one time, father, but now your requests would be in vain. I have lived with you, and I know that you will be able to get along without me.

MOIRANS: Find her a maid, and let her leave us in peace.

CLARISSE: Listen, father, will these be our farewells?

MOIRANS: Ah! (*He makes a gesture of despair.*)

CLARISSE: You will be happy, father, there are still so many beautiful landscapes in the world.

MOIRANS: You will not see them.

CLARISSE: We will travel in the summer.

MOIRANS: Your mother traveling! I can see that. (*A silence.*) One day ... perhaps we will reunite; if she ...

CLARISSE: If ... ? (*Understanding*) Even then we would not reunite.

MOIRANS: Why?

(*Clarisse does not answer and kneels*)

MOIRANS: You are praying. To whom are you praying? (*She does not answer; a long silence, then one hears the voice of Mrs. Moirans.*)

MRS. MOIRANS: (*whom one does not see*) Clarisse! Come see *The Paris News*. This would perhaps settle the search for a cook. Clarisse!

CURTAIN

(*August–September, 1913*)

ABOUT THE EDITORS

Dr. Brendan Sweetman is Professor of Philosophy and holds the Sullivan Chair in Philosophy at Rockhurst University, Kansas City, Missouri, USA. He is the author or editor of twelve books, including *The Vision of Gabriel Marcel* (Brill, 2008), and *A Gabriel Marcel Reader* (St. Augustine's Press, 2011). He has published more than one hundred articles and critical reviews in a variety of journals, collections, and reference works, including *International Philosophical Quarterly, American Catholic Philosophical Quarterly, Faith and Philosophy, Philosophia Christi, Philosophical Quarterly, Review of Metaphysics, New Catholic Encyclopedia, the Stanford Encyclopedia of Philosophy* and the *Encyclopedia Britannica*. Dr. Sweetman is the current President of the Gabriel Marcel Society, editor of *Marcel Studies*, Vice-President for North America of the World Conference of Catholic University Institutions of Philosophy (COMIUCAP), and an elected fellow of the *International Society for Science and Religion*. His books and articles have been translated into several languages, including Spanish, Portuguese and Italian.

Dr. Maria Traub holds the Doctor of Modern Language degree from Middlebury College, Vermont, where she specialized in French and Italian literature and language. She is currently Associate Professor of French and Italian at Neumann University, Aston, PA. In addition to her scholarly work at numerous conferences, Dr. Traub has translated many documents for individual researchers as well as for monasteries, including a file of correspondence between the Court of Versailles and notables of the American Revolution, including John Paul Jones, as research for Tim McGrath, *Give Me a Fast Ship: The Continental Navy and America's Revolution at Sea* (Caliber, 2014).

Dr. Geoffrey Karabin earned a licentiate degree from Katholieke Universiteit in Leuven, Belgium, and a Ph.D. in Philosophy from Villanova

University. He is Assistant Professor of Philosophy at Neumann University, Aston, PA. He has presented at numerous conferences and published on Marcel. Dr. Karabin's current research involves the relationship between a belief in immortality and violence. He is a co-founder and a member of the editorial board of *Marcel Studies*, a new journal dedicated to the thought of Gabriel Marcel.